FOOTBALL'S SECOND SEASON
Scouting High School Game Breakers

TOM LEMMING
with TAYLOR BELL

SPORTS PUBLISHING L.L.C.

SportsPublishingLLC.com

ISBN-13: 978-1-59670-209-7

Front cover photo by Getty Images/Rubberball

Publishers: Peter L. Bannon and Joseph J. Bannon Sr.
Senior managing editor: Susan M. Moyer
Editors: Jennine Crucet and Doug Hoepker
Art director: Dustin J. Hubbart
Dust jacket design: Dustin J. Hubbart
Project manager: Kathryn R. Holleman
Photo editor: Erin Linden-Levy

Sports Publishing L.L.C.
804 North Neil Street
Champaign, IL 61820
Phone: 1-877-424-2665
Fax: 217-363-2073
www.SportsPublishingLLC.com

Printed in the United States of America

    Library of Congress Cataloging-in-Publication Data

Lemming, Tom.
Football's second season : scouting high school game breakers / Tom
    Lemming and Taylor Bell.
        p. cm.
    Includes bibliographical references and index.
    ISBN 978-1-59670-209-7 (hard cover : alk. paper)
    1. Football–Scouting. 2. Football players–United States–Recruiting. 3.
    College sports–United States. I. Bell, Taylor H. A., 1940- II. Title.
    GV953.4.L46 2007
    796.332'62–dc22
                                    2007023512

CONTENTS

Foreword

IN MARCH OF 1980, coach Bo Schembechler hired me as an assistant football coach at the University of Michigan. He assigned me to recruit the Chicago area and it was my job to identify, evaluate, and recruit young men who possessed the myriad abilities necessary to succeed in the ultra-competitive environment that exists at Michigan.

One of the most difficult aspects of recruiting in that era was obtaining the game film or video needed to evaluate the recommended prospects from the hundreds of high schools that comprised this area. There was not enough time to visit every school in the four or five weeks allotted for spring recruiting, and the communication technology was not what it is today.

It was during this time that I first met Tom Lemming. Tom invited me, along with other college recruiters, to his home in Schaumburg to view the film and tapes he had collected from high school coaches throughout the Chicago area. He offered us a way to evaluate a lot of players in a short period, thus saving us valuable time. In the years to follow, hundreds of coaches would make their way to his home. Tom Lemming became a great resource to our recruiting efforts.

I liked him from the beginning; he was smart, honest, and I appreciated his love for the game and his passion for the

Tom Lemming, left, and Michigan coach Lloyd Carr.

recruiting process. He made a lot of friends in the coaching fraternity, both high school and college. He quickly became a respected media source who was always willing to relate his views and opinions on recruiting.

Before long he began to publish his evaluations and rankings of high school players. Next he began to rank college recruiting classes, which did not meet with the approval of many college coaches. Then he moved on to the national stage, touring the country by car in search of the nation's finest high school players. Then came the Internet; almost overnight, it seemed Tom Lemming was a big name. It was not overnight, of course, and it certainly was not always an easy ride.

Along the way he also met with controversy, most notably within the college coaching ranks and eventually with the NCAA. A college football coach is, by NCAA rule, allowed to make only a limited number of phone calls to a recruit. Tom

Lemming has no such restrictions and that allows him (and others in the field) the access that many coaches believe enables him undue influence in the recruiting process. This issue has resulted in concentrated efforts to limit his activities, but these efforts have had very little success. His perseverance and unyielding determination to chart and follow his own course have enabled him to scale the heights of his career.

Back in 1980, none of those who gathered at his home to watch film would have predicted that this "mailman" would become a revolutionary figure in the world of college football. Today, recruiting is college football's second season and—for better or worse—it has kept the passion of many college football fans burning during the winter months. In my judgment, more than anyone else, Tom Lemming has made it so.

As I look back on the impact he has had, what I see is a wonderful American story about a guy who followed his dream, and in the process, created a career and life that is successful beyond what anyone else could have imagined. It is a story about a guy who defied all odds and won. It is a story about a guy I admire a lot.

–LLOYD B. CARR

ANN ARBOR, MICHIGAN
FEBRUARY 2007

Preface

WHO'S TOM LEMMING?

FORMER MICHIGAN STATE FOOTBALL COACH George Perles used to refer to Tom Lemming as "the mailman." It was a backhanded reference to Lemming's other occupation at the time. How, Perles wondered, was Lemming qualified to evaluate high school prospects and recommend them to college recruiters? And why were they listening to a letter carrier?

Well, after a few years, Lemming finally convinced Perles. And he has delivered the goods to hundreds of other college coaches and football fanatics in the last 28 years. Lemming is, however, caught in a no-win situation. He probably would be booed at his own birthday party. You either love him or hate him—and that depends upon your college loyalty or what time of day it is. If you love him this year, the odds are better than 50/50 that you'll work up a good dislike for him in the next year or two. He is a lightning rod for controversy. That is the nature of his business—and he makes no apologies.

No, Lemming doesn't editorialize about politics or religion. He is a football recruiting analyst. He annually scouts the best high school players in the nation, both in person and on film, evaluating each before offering a "thumbs up" or "thumbs down," much like a movie critic. He publishes a national magazine that reports on the top 1,200 seniors, then responds when his opinions are challenged.

He has been doing his thing since 1978. No one else does it the same way—not then, not now. Tom Lemming is an original. Who else would drive 50,000 miles a year, from Seattle to Miami, sleep in his car, and eat tacos and cheeseburgers along the way, just to talk to thousands of teenage wannabes who dream of being the next John Elway? In his best-selling book, *The Blind Side: Evolution of a Game*, author Michael Lewis described Lemming, who is credited with discovering offensive lineman Michael Oher of Memphis, Tennessee, now a highly touted NFL prospect at the University of Mississippi, as "the only national football scout in America. Overnight, he became the leading independent authority on the subject of U.S. high school football players."

Bob Chmiel, who was recruiting coordinator at Northern Illinois, Northwestern, Michigan, and Notre Dame, said Lemming "does it better than anyone else in the country. He is thorough. He has no agendas. For every blue-chipper you read about, there is a kid you never heard about that Tom has helped to get to college. People don't know that side." Chmiel admits Lemming's candor is occasionally off-putting. "But if you criticize him, you don't know him," Chmiel says. "His heart is in the right place. He sincerely cares about the kids. He tells a kid what is best for him, and there are coaches who don't want to hear it. They are looking for a fall guy to explain why they didn't get a kid."

Not everybody is so complimentary. Type his name into a Google search engine and you'll quickly come to the understanding that he is respected and controversial, criticized and praised, ridiculed and admired by coaches, athletes, fans, and media alike. Critics wonder if Lemming has a personal agenda when it comes to his recruiting analysis. He says no: "I try to be as honest as possible."

I've known Lemming for 30 years, since my days covering high school sports for the *Chicago Daily News* and *Chicago Sun-Times.* If he can live with that answer, then so can I.

—TAYLOR BELL

CHICAGO, ILLINOIS
FEBRUARY 2007

INTRODUCTION

PREGAME WARMUP

WHEN I WAS TOLD THAT SOMEONE wanted to write a book about my career, I said no thanks. I didn't want to do it, in part because I didn't think people would want to read about me. I said no about 10 times before I was finally persuaded to say yes. And I'm still wondering if I made the right decision.

I am told I am at the top of the list in my profession. I only know that my position is unique. Name recognition has helped me to stay in the recruiting business nearly 30 years. I didn't have a magic wand or great connections when I was getting started. I came up the hard way. So it does make me feel good that I am now recognized. Still, when you are at the top, somebody will always try to shoot you down. Jealousy is everywhere in every walk of life, in every occupation, in every sport. I don't want to criticize other people. I don't want to say too many negative things. But I do want to respond to my critics, the ones who are jealous of what I have accomplished. I won't lie. I've never lied to a recruit, ever. So why lie to you?

I won't make much money from the publication of this book. But it will give me an opportunity to explain myself, to set the record straight on a lot of issues and to share things about me that people don't already know. Maybe after reading this book, those critics will understand where I am coming from, why I say some of the things I do, why I do some of the things I do. Possibly, they'll come to know me for my honesty and integrity, because that's what I have tried to maintain for the last 28 years. One college coach told me: "Why tell a recruit to go to college for an education, to the schools that graduate players? It hurts schools that don't graduate players." Well, because that's the truth.

I was the first to go out on the road and scout kids in their own back yards. Twenty-eight years later, I still am the only one who travels around the country to talk to kids. Where do the other recruiting analysts get their lists? From colleges that do their own scouting? From questionnaires distributed to high school coaches? Do they make their own determinations? They say I do it the wrong way. Well, what is the right way? Certainly not their way: purchasing lists and even charging recruits a monthly fee to write stories about them and show their videotapes. College recruiting is a *big* business.

In this book, I will talk about my journey from the beginning of the recruiting process in a behind-the-scenes approach. In the 1970s, there were a lot of backroom dealings. Now recruiting has become a sport in itself that rivals the actual season. I will show you how far it has come; I'll talk about the cheating that goes on, how college coaches sell their souls to land a blue-chip recruit; I'll discuss how I learned to evaluate prospects, and list all the players I missed as well as the players I discovered; and I'll walk you through how recruiting has evolved into a multimillion-dollar business.

I want to explain the way it was and the way it is—and my involvement in all of it. If I succeed, perhaps you will give me five stars. This time, you be the judge.

—TOM LEMMING

BARRINGTON, ILLINOIS
FEBRUARY 2007

FIRST QUARTER

1

WHAT RECRUITING IS ALL ABOUT

SOME SPORTSWRITERS HAVE ARGUED that college recruiting is a form of legalized prostitution. A coach solicits an athlete, wooing him with enticements such as a fully funded scholarship, a summer job, and an off-campus apartment . . . maybe even a car, a job for his father or mother, and free transportation to all games for his parents. It's the price of doing business. For colleges, recruiting is their lifeline. It's different than the National Football League. The NFL has a draft. In college, it's a caste system. The Super Sixteen programs usually have their pick of the top high school players. They are the rulers of the college system.

Who are those Super Sixteen? Notre Dame, Southern California, Texas, Oklahoma, Nebraska, Louisiana State, Alabama, Florida, Michigan, Ohio State, Florida State, Miami (Florida), Auburn, Georgia, Tennessee, and Penn State. They usually get—or at least compete for—who they want. The rest of the 117 schools in Division 1 are left to fend for themselves. The Super Sixteen are capable of recruiting nationally and beating local schools for local talent. It is an unfair system, but it is all we know.

The one constant in college football is that the Super Sixteen recruit the best players, then dominate the Top 10 rankings. It's rare for anyone else to break in. Recent exceptions have been Iowa, Clemson, UCLA, Washington, Colorado, Wisconsin, and Texas A&M. But for the most part, the rich get richer and the poor get poorer. The Super Sixteen prevail because they have a lot of factors in their favor: a winning tradition, rabid fans and alumni support, a king-sized stadium that seats 80,000 to 100,000 people, superior training facilities, and in the last 30 years, the slickest and most persuasive recruiters in the country.

To keep filling the seats and providing enough revenue to support the football program—and other men's and women's sports sponsored by the university—the elite teams must sign close to a Top 10 freshman class at least every other year. They must fill their needs by restocking their rosters with blue-chippers, players with speed and power who can become impact players, difference-makers. Each year schools bring in 20-25 players. A Super Sixteen school will try to bring in 20 blue-chippers—out of the top 250 in the nation—with the understanding that only 10 will make it. Ten won't make it because of injuries, poor grades, social problems, or other contributing factors. So with that in mind, a Super Sixteen school can't afford to sign a sub-par class two years in a row and risk falling behind the others.

Perception is the key word in all of recruiting. A class is rated not only by its talent level, but also by the perception it creates in the minds of wealthy alumni, fans, and the media. It is the hype surrounding recruiting classes that often dictates whether a program is on the right track. Two sub-par recruiting years in a row usually send up a red flag and signal a downward spiral that could be difficult for the coaches to overcome.

Things change quickly. For a program that is expected to win, one bad year can get the natives restless. For example, Michigan lost five games in 2005; that's not bad by many programs' standards, but Wolverine fans talked of ousting veteran coach Lloyd Carr, who had previously delivered the national championship that Bo Schembechler never could. It is that kind of mentality that placed so much pressure on Penn State's Joe Paterno when he struggled early this century, and on Florida State's Bobby Bowden, the winningest coach in college football history, when the Seminoles underperformed in 2006.

It's true that football recruiting isn't as bloodthirsty as it is in basketball. Recruits rarely go out on a limb anymore in basketball. Shoe companies dictate where the best basketball players go to school. And in college basketball, one great player can mean the difference between a Final Four team and a coaching change. Not so in football. One great freshman football recruit can't make the difference, at least not in one season. But that doesn't mean that there aren't plenty of cutthroat recruiting tactics in football. There were a lot of accusations tossed around in the 1970s and 1980s revolving around the illegal recruitment of players like Herschel Walker, Eric Dickerson, Marcus Dupree, and Hart Lee Dykes. Some were proven, most weren't. In several cases, it was presumed that a street agent or an influential, well-heeled alum made under-the-table payments or over-the-table propositions to a kid from a poor home, a kid without a father, a kid whose mother had no understanding of the recruiting process. It was all cloak and dagger, and it still goes on even today, just not to the extent that it does in basketball.

I have been evaluating high school football players for nearly three decades, so I've had plenty of time to observe the recruiting process. It's progressed from coaches sending recruits a postcard in the mail to coaches exchanging text messages with kids. Technology has certainly played its role. Now every major college has a website that covers recruiting, and the Internet is filled with recruiting services. In the early 1970s, there was no Internet, no *USA Today*, no summer camps, no videotapes, no Top 100 prospect lists, no frenzy over early commitments. Information wasn't readily available. Colleges subscribed to local newspapers around the country to find out about players. Or they relied on an alumni network to inform them about prospects in other areas.

Notre Dame was the only school that truly recruited nationally. For years, head coaches never went on the road to recruit before the season, and their assistants rarely traveled beyond a 300-mile radius of the school. Notre Dame, however, was the exception. Knute Rockne, who led Notre Dame to unprecedented dominance as head coach in the 1920s, brought in players from California, Texas, and New Jersey. He scheduled games against Army in New York's Yankee Stadium, played Southern California in Los Angeles, and Georgia Tech in Atlanta. With legendary sportswriter Grantland Rice penning, "Win one for the Gipper" stories, actor Pat O'Brien portraying Rockne in Hollywood's film version, and the "Four Horsemen" creating headlines, the Irish became American's Team and the darling of the media. Rockne worked off that notoriety to become a recruiting pioneer in college coaching.

The top colleges stockpiled players, offering 120 to 130 scholarships. Coaches signed three top quarterbacks just so two of them couldn't be recruited by their rivals. They would rather have amazing talent sit on their bench rather than suit up for the other team. When I began evaluating players in 1978, recruiting was still a hush-hush affair among college coaches. There was very little information—shared or otherwise—available on recruits. That's how the Super Sixteen liked it; the fewer competitors, the better. The NCAA had begun reducing scholarships from 105 to 95 to 85 over a four-year period. The major powers could no longer simply stockpile players as they once had done. So it was imperative for the Super Sixteen to shed very little light on the top incoming freshmen. Remember, freshmen weren't allowed to play until 1972. Today, if the NCAA were to prohibit freshmen from participating on the varsity level, recruiting websites would dry up, and fan and alumni enthusiasm would cool off. Schools, meanwhile, would complain that they don't have enough depth on their rosters to be competitive.

Smaller schools often argued back when I was starting out that the Super Sixteen had a huge advantage over everyone else. Those select schools could corner the market on the best prospects. But there wasn't a way to improve the system. Still isn't. You can't tell a kid where to go to school. And you can't conduct a draft. Some suggest the NCAA could further reduce the number of scholarships a school can offer to 70, and in the process create more parity in college football. But I believe the Super Sixteen and the other top 50 schools would still find a way to dominate.

When I began interviewing high school players and visiting college campuses from coast to coast in the 1970s, cheating was just about everywhere, and the NCAA was struggling to remain in any resemblance of control. It was the Wild, Wild West. There were few rules to monitor alumni, who befriended recruits both on and off the field, took them to dinner, arranged for jobs, and stuffed cash in their pockets. I took trips and talked to players and their parents. While being recruited, those players weren't inclined to talk about their relationships with colleges and alumni because they didn't want to kill the golden goose. I would pick up stories from teammates, friends, parents, and other players who were part of the recruiting process. Some of those stories were unfounded rumors, but others were factual. I came to realize that where there was smoke, normally there was fire. Eventually, off the record, I could uncover the truth from a player a few years later.

Cheating seemed to run absolutely rampant in the Southeast and Southwest conferences. In my opinion, a culture of cheating existed, where most coaches simply believed their competition was doing it and they didn't want to be caught at a disadvantage. When asked about it, those same coaches would accuse the opposition, deflecting blame elsewhere. Specifically, I recall hearing that certain schools were offering money to Eric Dickerson to sign with them. On signing day, Dickerson posed for a *Sporting News* picture in front of a new automobile while signing with Southern Methodist University, which was embroiled at the center of the debate. No one could prove anything in his case, but SMU was handed "the death penalty" by the NCAA a few years later for illegal recruiting violations. The school was banned from playing football for two years, and has been struggling to recover ever since.

The South did not hold exclusive rights to cheating. In the North, Illinois was keeping pace with SMU at the time. Several years after the celebrated slush fund scandal of the late 1960s forced Illinois to fire football coach Pete Elliott and basketball coach Harry Combes, the Illini were hit with another NCAA penalty, and football coach Mike White was fired in 1987.

Now, recruiting has become a cottage industry, a second season for fans and alumni who pin their hopes on the next class of recruits. Yet there are no exacts in recruiting, no won-loss record. In the South, with fewer professional teams, and the North, with cold weather, recruiting is a bridge and a lifeline between the football bowl games and the baseball season. In part, the public craze over recruiting is fueled by the sense of naiveté possessed by both recruits and fans. These are kids who can do no wrong. There used to be more heroes in sports, the John Elways and Dan Marinos, men without soiled reputations. With the rise in negative reporting and a higher tolerance for sarcasm, all the warts are revealed for everyone to see. It is very hard to find a hero who goes unscathed by the media. So in a way, these young kids provide us with what is often a false hope, of a new hero on the rise.

Fans are now much more involved in the recruiting process because of the Internet, which creates so much instant information. However, because of the anonymity of the Internet, a little man can flex his muscles on a web forum and spread hatred and untruths, which spoils the fun of sports and emphasizes that it's a business. Recruiting analysts pester high school kids on a regular basis, which is one reason why more and more recruits are choosing to commit early, to end the daily harassment. I certainly regret if I had anything to do with speeding up the process.

Still, despite the negatives, there isn't much that I don't like about recruiting.

2

MY ROOTS

I WOULD LIKE TO THINK that growing up on Chicago's South Side had a lot to do with my development as a human being and preparation for my career. But who prepares for a career as a football recruiting analyst? In the 1960s and 1970s, such a job didn't even exist. In those days, I collected baseball cards and wanted to work for the Chicago Cubs.

Well, it never happened. I called Vedie Himsl, the Cubs' director of scouting. "Could I come down for an interview?" I asked. "No," he told me. So I went to Wrigley Field to see Bob Kennedy, the general manager. He never saw me, but I did speak with Himsl, who laughed when I said I wanted to be a scout. He gave me the old "Don't call us, we'll call you" response. So for the next year, I called Himsl every month to see if there were any openings. I told him I'd do anything, even sweep floors, to get my foot in the door. Finally, after baseball turned a deaf ear to me, I decided to go into football recruiting, because I could call my own shots. It wasn't my first choice, but I had no other options.

I had read a column by Dave Condon of the *Chicago Tribune* that mentioned a guy named Joe Terranova from Dearborn, Michigan, who at the end of that year (1976) had rated the best college football recruiting classes. (Penn State was ranked No. 1.) The whole thing intrigued me, and the following spring I called Terranova and asked if I could come to his house to talk recruiting. He was very gracious, especially considering I was a neophyte. But he had only been doing it for two years, he told me. He never contacted players or watched film, so his methods were very different. In those days, 16-millimeter film reels were too bulky to mail, so in lieu of scouting trips and visual aids, he simply gathered his information from coaches at Notre Dame, Michigan, and a few other schools.

We sipped iced tea in his backyard and talked recruiting. He advised me not to try to do what he did for a full-time job. He was an executive at Ford Motor Company and didn't think anyone could make a full-time living by analyzing football players. He didn't discourage me, but he didn't encourage me, either. Later, I did receive encouragement from Gerry Faust, who at that time was the famous coach of Cincinnati's Moeller High School (before coaching at Notre Dame). Faust told me he didn't know of anyone who was filling the role I hoped to fill. He fed me suggestions for players to scout, and I began watching games involving those players while also reading whatever stories I could from newspapers in Chicago, Detroit, St. Louis, Pittsburgh, and the like.

That's how I got started. But it wasn't the beginning. I was born on September 25, 1954, in St. Anthony's Hospital in Chicago. My family lived in an apartment building at 33rd and Ashland, not far from old Comiskey Park. My father, Tom, was born and raised in Chicago. He dropped out of high school in 1929, during the Depression. He later became a World War II hero, earning four bronze star medals before being wounded in North Africa. He then worked as a truck driver and died of cancer in 1984. My mother, Edie, was a housewife who died of lung cancer in 1996. Our four-room apartment was tight on space and had to accommodate six people: me; my parents; my sister, Kathleen, who works in newspaper advertising and lives in Orland Park; my brother, Terry, a lieutenant in the Illinois State Police; and my brother, Tim, a U.S. Army veteran who retired after 20 years and now works for the Georgia State Police.

When I was seven years old, we moved into a three-bedroom brick bungalow in central Stickney, more commonly referred to as Sahs, a half-square-mile tract of unincorporated Chicago. Midway Airport was five blocks south of our house. We grew accustomed to the noise to the point where we didn't even notice. It was a rather poor neighborhood. Laramie, a major North-South thoroughfare, was one of the dividing streets between Stickney and Chicago. The Chicago side of Laramie was paved, but the Stickney side was tar and gravel. That was true for all of the streets in Stickney, which remained unpaved until the mid-1960s. It was a unique setting to grow up in. My family was Irish, but a lot of Polish immigrants lived in our neighborhood, and many of them didn't speak English.

It could be a rough, racist neighborhood, too. During the 1960s, two black families moved into homes on Central Avenue. Their homes caught fire, and the volunteer fire department didn't show up in time to put out the blaze. My parents didn't condone such attitudes, though. They were enlightened, and they liked everyone. The crime in the neighborhood appalled them, but they didn't wear their feelings on their sleeves. As I think back to those times, I believe a lot of their values rubbed off on me.

My father worked extremely hard to keep our family going—two jobs without any vacation. Our family never saw Dad between six o'clock in the morning and eight o'clock at night. On most nights after a long day of work he would unwind with friends at Little Canada, a tavern in central Stickney, with a few drinks and a pack of cigarettes. I don't drink to this day, because my father drank too much. That was his only weakness. Otherwise, he was a great father and husband, an old-fashioned man who was tough as nails.

I attended Charles J. Sahs elementary school at 50th and Long. Much of the tax money from local businesses went to support our elementary school, which was among the richest schools in the state. It had an Olympic-sized swimming pool, the latest athletic equipment, and new books.

I had never played sports until I enrolled at Sahs, where nearly everyone was interested in athletics. We played baseball on unpaved streets and tackle football on an asphalt field with snow on the ground. I also played basketball, captaining a team called Lemming's Lemons in eighth grade. But I never cared much for basketball, or even football, which I played because I was the fastest kid in Stickney. All of my attention was given to baseball, and by the time I was 14 I had quit all other sports. Baseball was the love of my young life. I recall the old right-handed softball mitt that was our household's lone glove. I was a lefty, and when I was young I would have to field the ball with that glove on my left hand, then remove it to throw to first base. Eventually, my father bought me a left-handed glove.

I was a pretty good player, always one of the best in our neighborhood. Instead of playing high school baseball at Reavis High School, I decided to play in the Connie Mack League for 14-to-17-year-olds. Baseball wasn't a popular sport at the school, so I opted out. In Connie Mack ball, I was named most valuable player in the Vittum Park league when I was 17. I played center field and stole eight bases in one game. My only problem was my right eye, which is close to legally blind. I am a natural lefty, but my right eye made hitting left-handed too difficult, so I switched to the right-handed side of the batter's box when I was 15.

My dream of playing center field for the Cubs consumed me in the summertime. I would play baseball in the morning at Sahs Park, go home and bounce a rubber ball off the back of our brick bungalow to improve my reflexes, watch the Cubs on television, then go to Vittum Park for a game or practice. Nothing compared to actually sitting in Wrigley Field, though, so I had a newspaper route to earn enough money to attend Cubs games. Without telling my parents, I'd walk to Archer Avenue, take a bus to downtown Chicago, then take the El (or

"L," short for elevated train) to Wrigley Field and buy a bleacher seat. All the while, my parents thought I was at practice. I saw at least 15 games every summer and got to meet Stan Musial, Roberto Clemente, Sandy Koufax, Tom Seaver, and Pete Rose. The greatest Cubs game I remember was on my 12th birthday—September 25, 1966. My hero at the time, Kenny Holtzman, pitched that day, a complete-game, two-hit performance as the Cubs defeated Koufax's Dodgers, 2-1. As a bonus, I got Holtzman to sign my program.

In those days, every boy dreamed of being a batboy for his favorite team. The Cubs only seemed to let rich kids be batboys. But the White Sox conducted a contest, asking kids to respond to the question: "Why do you want to be a White Sox traveling batboy?" I wrote a long letter and waited for them to call, fantasizing about making a trip with the White Sox to the east coast. But I never got a call.

Still, nothing could persuade my mind to wander too far from baseball. Like most kids my age, I collected baseball cards. I memorized the backs of every Cubs baseball card— when the players were born, their major-league statistics, even their minor-league stats. I guess you could say I was obsessed with names and numbers even then. I also memorized the names of each of the 181 Texans who were killed at the Alamo, the Gettysburg Address, and a good part of the U.S. Constitution. My fifth grade teacher, Mrs. Kuehn, said it was a waste of time to memorize those things, and that I should spend my time on something more useful. She probably was right. (But then again, having a good memory helps me in my business.) Despite my memorization abilities, I was just an average student. The only book I ever brought home to read was a history book, as American history was my second love.

As a high school senior, my dreams of making the majors finally came to a crashing halt. I was only 5-foot-10 and 160 pounds as an 18-year-old, too small to garner attention from any major-league scouts. With my hopes dashed, I focused on going to college. I wanted to attend Western Illinois University to major in communications or history. If I couldn't play center field for the Cubs, I wanted to be a sports broadcaster or sportswriter—really, I just wanted to be involved in sports. But my family couldn't afford to send me to college, and my grades simply weren't good enough to earn me an academic scholarship. So college was out of the question, too.

I worked as a printer at an envelope company, as an Andy Frain usher at Cubs and White Sox parks, and as a waiter at a dinner playhouse. I saved my money throughout my senior year, while trying to fend off the negative feedback I was receiving from others. Certainly, no one was going to volunteer to knock down any doors to help me. My high school guidance counselor said I should forget about my dream of being a broadcaster. His alternative was for me to work on the docks or become an electrician or truck driver.

I actually saved enough money so I could follow my brother, Terry, to college. He received a master's degree in criminology at Western Illinois. But when the time came to spend that money on a college education, I instead decided to spend it on a different sort of education: traveling around Europe. My parents were against it, but I went overseas anyway with a friend, Ralph Schiller, a Reavis graduate who was attending Loyola University in Chicago. We ran out of money earlier than expected and so I came home. But I enjoyed my travel so much that I worked for another year and saved enough money to go back to Europe. I took three overseas trips in total, and with each trip I found reasons why I shouldn't go to college. I visited every country in Europe, and traveled as far East as Turkey and Russia and as far south as Northern Africa. I saw the Pyramids, the Kremlin, the Eiffel Tower, and the Parthenon. For someone in love with history, it was a thrill.

I knew, however, that I couldn't travel forever. I started thinking about my future, or more precisely whether I had one. Having blown my education money, I was left with little in the way of options. So there I was, in the summer of 1977, sitting on the bank of the Nile River in Egypt wondering what to do with my life. "I could be a scout for the Cubs," I thought to myself. "Or I could start a Cubs newsletter." At the time, I had no money to do anything, but I was eager to try.

So after I was rejected by the Cubs, and after I had met Joe Terranova and was encouraged by Gerry Faust and later Joe Kozak, the sports editor at the Chicago Catholic newspaper, to consider football scouting, I began to put a game plan together. I was going to be a football scout, and I couldn't wait to get started.

3

MY GAME PLAN

JOE TERRANOVA HAD A GOOD IDEA. And college coaches—always looking for talent wherever they can find it—purchased his report. After all, no one else was doing what he was doing, even to the limited extent that he was doing it. But I wanted to do it differently, in a more detailed fashion.

At the time, I was living in Lombard, one of Chicago's western suburbs, and stringing for a few suburban weekly newspapers, covering football games and submitting reports. But that was soon to change. In November 1977, I designed a blueprint for the 1978 season to evaluate the class of 1979. My game plan was, and still is, to provide fans and college coaches with as much information as possible regarding the top 1,200 high school players in the country. The goal is to complete an up-close-and-personal look at each prospect through seeing them in person and on film. It was a unique approach in 1978, and to this day, no one else does it that way.

As I reflect on how it all began, I never wavered in the belief that I was going to make a living out of something I really enjoyed. My only frustration stemmed from how long it took to finally get my head above water. I didn't start to make money until my seventh year in 1986. Most people would have given up by then. Maybe I was just a stubborn Irishman. I never took out a bank loan or borrowed a penny from anyone, adhering to a philosophy of independence learned from my father. He taught me never to buy anything unless I had the money to pay for it. So to earn money for my trips, I worked at an envelope company. I was on a tight budget while on the road, sleeping in my car rather than staying in budget hotels. I did whatever it took to meet my goal of scouting those 1,200 players.

That first year, I became the first person to interview high school players across the nation, not just in one area. I wanted my reports to be more personal, like a reporter. My idea was to outwork everyone else, and I had tunnel vision. I yearned to be successful, the first proven, respected national football recruiting analyst. Even if I met that goal, I still had no idea if I could make a living in that profession. But I was determined to do everything I could to make it work—or die trying.

I had no connections. And knowing the people who know people is the most important aspect of my business. So from the outset, colleges turned their backs on me. Michigan's Bo Schembechler wouldn't talk to me. Notre Dame's Dan Devine wouldn't talk to me. Neither would Ohio State's Earle Bruce nor Penn State's Joe Paterno. Schembechler first heard about me in 1979, and I believe he thought I was from Mars. "You're doing *what?*" he asked. He was old school, and I think it upset him that I was talking to all these players. Other coaches were the same way, worrying that I would somehow hurt their recruiting efforts.

In those days, recruiting was a very clandestine operation. One coach knew little about what his competition was doing and who they were after. When I started writing about everyone and releasing it to a national audience, all this new information was introduced. Not just to coaches, but to kids, too. A star player in California could suddenly read up on where a star player from Pennsylvania was leaning toward going to college. Kids began to educate themselves about the recruiting process. They learned, "Hey, I'm not the only blue-chipper in the region." This opened up a dialogue between recruits, who would then swap recruiting stories and share insights into unfamiliar programs.

I recall one meeting in Wheaton, Illinois, in 1981, with high school star Jim Juriga, one of the most highly touted offensive linemen in the country and later a standout at Illinois. At the meeting, Juriga pointed out that one college had singled him out as its No. 1 priority for that year. But another player I had written about had said the same college had told him that he was its No. 1 priority. Yet another player said the same thing. It became clear to Juriga that he was being fed a line, which was a great insight into the recruiting process.

For me, doors slowly began to open. The first coach to lend a helping hand was George McIntyre of Vanderbilt. His chief recruiter, Dave Roberts—who later was head coach at Baylor, offensive coordinator at Notre Dame, and an assistant to Lou Holtz at South Carolina—allowed me to sit in on film sessions that Vanderbilt conducted. With experience and help, I gained confidence in my own ability to evaluate talent. Along the way, I gained more friendships with college coaches. Once reluctant to talk to me, many coaches were now opening their doors. Today, as many as 50 coaches per week stop by my house to watch film during the May evaluation period. It's been one amazing about-face from my roots in 1978.

As a young scout, I relied on newspapermen from Chicago, Cincinnati, and Detroit to publicize my efforts, and I did interviews on radio stations to attract subscribers to my newsletter. I had only one subscriber in 1979, my first year. Don Mankin of Oak Park, Illinois, saw my name in a *Chicago Sun-Times* article. I was embarrassed that only one person in this big country of ours saw fit to subscribe to my newsletter, so instead of taking his money, I sent him a free magazine. To this day, he continues to receive a free subscription.

I used up a lot of youthful energy and exuberance during my travels early in my career. What I lacked in business savvy or knowledge—I did a lot of things without thinking them out—I made up for with effort and restraint. I had to be economical, so I planned trips east of the Mississippi River and north of the Alabama and Mississippi state lines, no farther south than Chattanooga, Tennessee. I chose Chattanooga only because I wanted to see Lookout Mountain, site of one of the great battles of the Civil War. My travel restrictions dictated that I speak with Eric Dickerson in Sealy, Texas, and John Elway in Granada Hills, California, over the phone rather than in person. They were the two biggest names on a list of more than 100 players I called because I couldn't visit. I fed pay phones—which was cheaper than calling from home—to speak to those recruits, dropping in additional quarters after three minutes so I would not be cut off when the time ran out.

Eric Dickerson was a huge name in 1978, the No. 2 player in the nation, behind John Elway and ahead of Dan Marino. He was a big running back—"The best since Oklahoma's Billy Sims," people were saying. No running back had what Eric Dickerson had—that great combination of size and speed—until Herschel Walker came along the following year, then Bo Jackson and Marcus Dupree in the next four years. I called Dickerson's high school and talked to his coach, who then put Dickerson on the phone. I told him my name was Tom Lemming of *Prep Football Report*. I asked him which schools he was considering, and what football players he compared himself to. It wasn't a very enlightening conversation. Kids are always soft-spoken when they don't know the interviewer, so that person has to drag things out of them. It's even more difficult to do that when talking on the phone instead of eye to eye. That's why I prefer to meet in person.

I like to sit down with a player, watch around 15 minutes of game film, and get a reaction from him. It helps me to understand what the player is feeling as he is making a run or a tackle. A player's true emotions come out when he watches himself on film. You can't get that feeling over a phone call, and it really is the basis for a sound judgment on the kid's personality. It is also invaluable to have the coach in the room. He lends his expertise about the player, and the coach will usually provide me with an honest appraisal. From the coach, I can find out about the player's leadership skills, his drive both on and off the field, and some background on the kid's family.

I still interview about 200 players in this manner each year. I can't be that extensive with all 1,200 kids I interview during my trips, but I am for the best of the best. I'm the only person, including college coaches, who meets with those 200 players in such a setting. That's how I am able to accurately compare kids and pick a worthy All-America team. Right or wrong, I've seen and spoken to them all.

The first player I interviewed in person was Dan Marino. His high school was located near Pitt Stadium on the University of Pittsburgh campus. Western Pennsylvania was loaded with great players at the time, and Marino was just one of many prospects from the area I was scouting during a recruiting weekend. Marino's high school coach told me that Marino would be at Pitt Stadium that day, along with several of the other prospects I had hoped to scout. Marino was the most athletic looking player of the lot; already he looked like an NFL quarterback, and he was clearly a leader. He had a great arm and superb release, and he had a bearing about him that I rarely have seen, especially from a kid so young. He just had an aura about him. There was no doubt that he was a Hall of Famer in training.

The other amazing quarterback I scouted that year was John Elway, who at a young age was already very media savvy and easy to talk to on the phone. His father was a college coach who had coached at San Jose State and later at Stanford. John never bragged about his heritage or himself, though. He was being recruited by Notre Dame, USC, and Michigan, but he chose to attend Stanford. He was a large, athletic kid, probably the most athletic quarterback I have ever seen. On film, he resembled a larger-than-life Fran Tarkenton.

Roger Craig from Davenport, Iowa, was in my top 10 that year, too, as was Chattanooga's Reggie White. My choice as the best defensive player in the country wasn't Reggie White, the future NFL Hall of Famer, however; it was George Achica of San Jose, California, who went to USC. The class of 1979—the high school seniors who played in 1978—included a roster of future stars: Elway; Dickerson; Marino; Achica; White; Craig; tight end Tony Hunter of Cincinnati Moeller, who went to Notre Dame; defensive end Joey Browner of Atlanta, and offensive tackle Don Mosebar of Visalia, California, who both attended USC; offensive tackle Irv Eatman of Dayton, Ohio, who chose UCLA; defensive lineman Mike Carter of Dallas, who went to SMU; and running back Jimmy Smith of Kankakee, Illinois, who selected Purdue. Not a bad list for Year One.

4

LEARNING THE BIZ

A BIG PART OF MY LIFE is spent answering questions from disgruntled parents who don't understand the recruiting process. They want to know why their son, who was an All-State selection, isn't receiving scholarship offers from Division I schools. I answered them, of course, but it took a long time before I could give them what I felt was a truly honest and accurate answer. Like the athletes and their parents, I was still in the process of educating myself. And unfortunately for me, the best teachers—college coaches—wouldn't speak to me. I begged to be invited to visit them on campus and watch film with them. But no coach at a powerhouse program would give me the time of day.

Now I realize that if I were in their shoes, I probably wouldn't talk to me, either. What benefit would they gain by talking to me about their players or their recruits? Why would they bother to divulge their evaluating and recruiting secrets to a stranger? So I shifted my focus to the smaller football schools with coaches who were more eager to teach me a thing or two about recruiting: Vanderbilt, Purdue, Indiana, Wisconsin, Iowa State, Temple, and Boston College.

The first person to lend a hand was Dave Roberts, then an assistant at Vanderbilt under head coach George McIntyre. Roberts was recruiting the Chicago area and figured if he scratched my back, I'd scratch his. We compared notes on players I had met on my travels, and in turn he was completely honest with me. Roberts and other members of the Vanderbilt staff would collect 16mm films from Chicago-area schools in the mornings and afternoons, then sit in a room at their suburban hotel at night and watch one film after another. Looking over Dave's shoulder, I learned how to break down film and evaluate players. The coaches showed me what skills they were looking for at each position, and taught me how to identify the genuine prospects with potential to play at the top level of college ball. I kept my mouth shut and soaked it all in.

Later, Illinois coach Mike White and his staff did the same thing for me, setting up shop in a two-room suite at a suburban Chicago hotel. They would have five film projectors spinning at the same time, as I scrambled to keep up with the frenetic pace. What did I learn? Plenty. Roberts had a rule of thumb that I've found to be a pearl of wisdom: If a high school kid looks great on film, normally he will be a great college player, regardless of size or speed. A kid might look like an NFL player, but size and muscles aren't everything. Some kids pass the eye test, but they can't play the game. Others can play the game, even if they don't appear to have the necessary strength.

College coaches know that if a player has the frame, production, and speed, they can build him up strength-wise with superb strength coaches and weight-training facilities. That's why a 6-foot-7, 260-pound offensive lineman may be a hot recruit, despite lacking some of the desired strength in high school. The kid may only bench press 240 pounds, but if he can bend his knees and move his feet well then he will be heavily recruited.

Evaluating talent requires a scout to compare one quarterback to another, rather than comparing a quarterback to a running back. It sounds obvious, but you must compare apples to apples, one position to the same position. I feel like I have good instincts when it comes to judging quarterbacks, determining that player's arm strength, the fluidity of his motion, and how quickly he finds open receivers. But I'm still not in the same class with Nebraska's Bill Callahan, Notre Dame's Charlie Weis, or Tennessee's David Cutcliffe when it comes to quarterbacks. Those guys are the best.

When evaluating running backs, size doesn't matter as much as instincts, cutting ability, good vision, and great quickness, which is different than great speed. As for wide receivers, in the old days, they had to be small and explosive. Now recruiters are looking for tall, large-handed receivers with explosive speed, athletes who can present mismatches against shorter defensive backs. Randy Moss and Terrell Owens are perfect examples of this ideal, as they have soft hands, make pass-receiving look easy, and can take off after catching the ball.

Linebackers must feature superb lateral quickness, speedy feet, and the sort of flexibility needed to drop back into passing lanes effortlessly. College coaches look for leadership ability from this position. The next Dick Butkus or Lawrence Taylor must be in on almost every play in high school or he likely won't be a great college player.

Defensive backs must be the best athletes on the field. An elite defensive back must be able to turn his hips and run backwards as fast as receivers run forward. Today, the demand is for them to be taller because receivers are also taller. It is very difficult to find defensive backs who have enough athleticism to play with tall wide receivers.

I've always believed that cornerbacks and defensive linemen are the toughest positions to fill because the athletic ability required goes a long way in determining who is capable of playing those spots. Defensive linemen must have size but not at the expense of athleticism. They also must have an aggressive nature and explosive speed, something that big guys normally lack.

While defensive linemen are tougher to find than offensive linemen, the toughest position to evaluate is offensive linemen. First of all, it's difficult to find good game film on them. Everybody has film on quarterbacks and running backs. But offensive linemen? Good luck. Linemen must have great size (nowadays, 6-foot-6, 300 pounds is good for starters), quick feet, above-average body control, and flexible legs.

Sometimes a player who excelled in high school doesn't make the cut in college. For example, a 5-foot-9 nose guard will not make it in Division I football, no matter how many sacks he had in high school. Similarly, a Division I team won't recruit a running back who rushes for 2,000 yards but covers 40 yards in only 4.8 seconds. A prospect can be undersized or not quite as quick as the profile demands, but he can't miss by too much.

That's the school's perspective, however. I don't always agree with that. I've watched over 20,000 films in the last 28 years, so I've become somewhat of an expert in evaluating a player through film—and it's important to note that I'm speaking of *game* film, not a film of *highlights*. I've learned what specifically separates the great from the greatest. I place a lot of weight on a player's performance in games. I think performance is a better indicator of future success than size and speed. If a kid is a great talent in high school but maybe a bit slow or undersized for his position, I still recommend him to colleges, because if he performs in an outstanding manner at the high school level, I think he'll also be productive in college.

"Performance" is subjective to some degree. But you know it when you see it. It's a kid who stands out, makes plays, is a difference-maker—someone you notice right away. A good example was Tim Jamison of Thornton Township in Harvey, Illinois, a Chicago suburb. He went to Michigan and was a member of the Wolverines' outstanding defensive unit in 2006.

The first time I saw Jamison was during a Thornton game versus Bolingbrook. I was there to scout Bolingbrook's touted linebacker Kyle Williams, who later signed with Purdue, and quarterback Marcus Randle El, brother of NFL player Antwaan Randle El, who attended Wisconsin. I didn't know who Jamison was prior to the game. Standing on the Bolingbrook sideline, I was blown away by this hard-hitting kid who had quickness to the ball and awesome awareness. I hadn't seen a kid hit like that in 10 years. His name, of course, was Tim Jamison. He wasn't on anyone's radar before that game, but now he was on mine.

On the flip side of the coin is Kyle Williams, the player I was there to see. Williams was rated among the Top 25 players in the nation by one recruiting service. In the game, though, he made only two tackles and was outperformed by his teammate, Ryan Bain, who was credited with a dozen tackles. Williams had obvious size and speed, the kind of player who could perform well at a combine. But in game action, he faded into the background. Still, I thought Bain was a fluke. I needed a second opinion, so I went to see him in another game, and, once again, he outplayed Williams.

Bain was 6-foot-2 and 250 pounds at that time, and he had a motor that didn't quit. He was tough and aggressive and very productive, and after two games, I came away a believer. I added him to my All-America team as a defensive tackle. Bain's favorite school was Notre Dame, but the Fighting Irish told him that he couldn't play for them, noting a lack of size to play defensive tackle. So he opted for Iowa.

As I gained experience as a scout, I eventually learned to not fall in love solely with physical attributes and ignore the Bains of high school football. For my first 15 years, I penalized kids for lack of size or speed even though when I looked at them on film, they appeared dynamic and were very productive. Then I changed my mind. I had been proven wrong in far too many cases, including obvious ones like Barry Sanders, Bill Romanowski, Mike Alstott, and Drew Brees. I decided that productivity was more important as long as a prospect was close to the required standards for size and speed. I'm not going to recommend a 5-foot-6 offensive lineman for a Division I roster, but if a player is in the ballpark, I'll give him the benefit of the doubt if his performance on the field merits it.

There's also the "intangibles" to consider: How bad does this kid want to win? A scout can't always accurately answer that question simply by watching a kid on the field. That's why I find it important to talk to kids. I always ask each player similar questions driving at the same goal: to find out what role athletics—and football in particular—play in a kid's life. "How important is football to you?" I'll ask each kid. His response to that one question could change him from a 3-star player to a 4-star player, when taken into consideration with his abilities on the field. Or, it could have the opposite effect, and his rating could suffer.

I recall John Foley's desire as being second to none. He was a linebacker at St. Rita High School in Chicago, who was named the *Chicago Sun-Times* Player of the Year in 1985. He went to Notre Dame and was destined for stardom before an arm injury curtailed his promising career. Foley lived his whole life for football. He loved the game—couldn't live without it. To him, the game wasn't a means to an end or a chore he had to put up with; football absolutely consumed him. Those are the sort of guys I look for on a daily basis.

Another player who reminds me of Foley is Tommy Zbikowski, a quarterback at Buffalo Grove, Illinois, High School. He was the *Chicago Sun-Times* Player of the Year in 2002, and he became one of the hardest-hitting and most aggressive safeties in college football for Notre Dame. I believe I was the only analyst who ranked Zbikowski in the top 100. He had great speed—running 100 meters in 10.6 seconds—but lacked some size and experience, having played very little at the defensive back position in high school. Tommy was 5-foot-11 and weighed 180 pounds. Not many college coaches would recruit a quarterback with those credentials. (At Notre Dame, he was switched from cornerback to safety after one day of practice.) But when I watched him play and spoke to him, I noticed he had an unbelievable love for contact and competition, so he made my list.

I also ask players to fill out questionnaires to obtain information on how they've fared in other sports, as well as how they performed in the classroom and on college-entrance exams. In the recruiting process, one of the first things a college coach wants to see is a player's transcript. Does he qualify for my university? If not, a college can't waste time recruiting a player, no matter how good he is.

The questions don't end there. I also pepper each kid with questions about his health and medical history. Has he had any previous injuries? If so, when was he injured? It's possible that I watched a game tape of a player and thought he looked poorer than expected. Maybe that was due to a knee injury that he had not fully recovered from. Was that injury affecting his production? These are the sort of questions that I find imperative to ask, to make certain that my report is thorough.

So, it's easy to see that there's a lot to consider when scouting a kid. Still, sometimes scouting is too easy. There will always be no-brainers like Jonathan Stewart, Adrian Peterson, and Jimmy Clausen—kids that are the total package and perform like it on the field. When I first saw Stewart, from Lacey, Washington, he was already well known. It was a great year for running backs in 2004, a class that produced at least 12 elite players at that position, and I saw them all. But Stewart was the best of the bunch. No one rated him as highly as I did, but, in my view, he clearly deserved to be at the top of the list. He had size, speed, production, and great vision. As a 5-foot-10, 220-pound senior in high school, he averaged over 10 yards per carry, bench pressed 360 pounds, and ran 100 meters in 10.5 seconds. Now Stewart is a big star at Oregon. He isn't in a class with Herschel Walker or Eric Dickerson or

Marcus Dupree or Bo Jackson. But he belongs in the next tier. Since he is at Oregon and not USC, he won't command as much national publicity. But if you are a truly great talent, the NFL will find you eventually.

And so will I. My percentage of hits has far outweighed my percentage of misses over the past 15 years, all due to my willingness to adapt my scouting strategy and place more emphasis on results.

5

PREP FOOTBALL REPORT

MY ORIGINAL GAME PLAN was to be the first to publish a Chicago Cubs newsletter, the forerunner of today's *Vine Line*. But the Cubs weren't interested at the time, so I launched my own football newsletter instead. There seemed to be more interest in college football than professional football at the time. Some college football programs were so secretive concerning their recruiting that they delayed the announcement of their incoming freshman classes several weeks after the signing day. This created a lot of expectation from fans, who wanted to know what was going on. Recognizing that market, I pounced on it with my newsletter.

In 1979, I published my first *Prep Football Report.* I printed four issues during that first year, but each issue was only eight pages long. The girlfriend of my good friend Floyd Wisner handled the typing duties. My subscriber list featured but one name, so I advertised the newsletter on six radio stations to try to attract interest. The response wasn't as immediate as I had hoped. But I had big ambitions. I knew I would suffer financially in the first few years, as I tried to convince people it was worth the asking price.

People wanted to read my newsletter, but they didn't want to pay for it. I lost $4,000 to $5,000 that first year due to travel expenses, and the debt was certainly of concern. On several occasions during the first three years, I thought about giving up and getting a real job. But each time I persuaded myself to stick it out; I continued working on the side to save money for my recruiting trips.

Eventually, that faith and persistence paid off—big time. *Prep Football Report* has expanded from eight to its current 300 pages. By 1983, when I crossed the Mississippi River for the first time on my annual scouting trip, the circulation had reached nearly 1,000 subscribers. In 1990, when I was driving through every state in the Union except Alaska, Hawaii, and North Dakota, the paid readers numbered 4,000.

My big report is published on August 1 every year. I also write two 60-page magazines in January and March, and publish five eight-page newsletters during the year, in April, June, September, October, and November. In the large report, I evaluate 1,200 to 1,500 players and include 600 to 700 pictures. As an added bonus, I include a travel story, detailing virtually every mile of every trip I made during the year—a travelogue of my coast-to-coast odyssey. Eat your heart out, Rick Steves.

I start in December with the magazine. After each trip from December to June, I dictate every scrap of information and each interview into a tape recorder. Then those tapes are transcribed by Michelle Abell, a graphic designer and professional typist with Abell-Written Communications. She is the fastest typist I have ever seen, plus she rarely makes a mistake. So she's been my reliable aid for the past 15 years.

After all my travels are complete and the tapes are transcribed, I then take some time to reflect on everything I've seen that year. I wait as long as possible—usually until the week before the final product goes to the printer—to compile my rankings. By that time, I have all the necessary information I need, and I can be sure that my decision is thoughtful and informed.

As for the cover design of the magazine, I've been taking group pictures for publication since my very first year, but the magazine was printed in black and white until 1990, when I could finally afford to make the switch to full color. On each cover, I attempt to combine American history, such as renowned campus sites, with sports history. I aim to make each cover uniquely different, a reflection of my interest in history and my love for the sport. I always try to have the players positioned in front of a spot where you wouldn't expect them to be, and it generally produces an interesting photo.

I've received a lot of favorable comments about the covers, but I owe much of that to the players who line up to be photographed. I thought the 2005 cover, with the Alamo in the background, was the best of all. The picture featured 15 All-Americans, including quarterbacks Mitch Mustain, Tim Tebow, and Matt Stafford; wide receiver Percy Harvin; and defensive back Myron Rolle.

The main reason people pick up my magazine is for my rankings, my own thorough evaluations of the top prospects. The prospects who have more hype I spend plenty of time scouting before I offer my evaluation. Take quarterback Jimmy Clausen, for example. He was a consensus choice among scouts as the No. 1 high school player in the country in 2006. Before I came to my own determination about Clausen, I watched each of his game films from his sophomore and junior years. It's necessary to spend that kind of time on the great ones if I am going to accurately rank them in my top 100.

But I also spend a lot of time scouting kids who aren't considered to be Division I prospects. I have over 1,000 films sent to me from parents or kids who want me to evaluate them. I feel obligated to look at some of each and every film I receive, and then give an honest appraisal. Every once in a while, I find a kid who is worth considering for my list.

All this work means a lot to me: *Prep Football Report* is my pride and joy, and I value the integrity of the product. I'm not bragging, but I don't believe anyone else publishes a book like this, so exact and so detailed. I write every word and take every picture. There isn't anything in the magazine that doesn't have my stamp on it.

Putting together the *Report* is a backbreaking, arduous task to say the least. I have to be healthy every year and must keep that inner drive alive. The natural competitor in me comes out on a daily basis, as I strive to scoop the competition with accurate, well-researched reporting and sound opinion. In the era of instant news, I have been able to stay competitive because I have a unique approach to scouting that hasn't been challenged or compromised in three decades.

◆　　◆　　◆

Now, about that list. . . . When deciding where a player will end up in my rankings, I have to look beyond my evaluation of the player's skills, size, strength, and statistics, to also consider the competition level he has faced. A kid can average 13 yards per carry, but is he doing that against stiff competition, or is he playing against Little Sisters of the Poor? Knowing the talent level of the competition is key. Then I can form an educated opinion on whether the prospect will dominate when faced with a playing field that is his equal. For me to consider a prospect worthy of making my top 100 list, that player can't just be good—he must be dominating to be a true All-American.

As I weed down my list, forcing it to shrink by leaps and bounds, I'll attempt to break down a player's abilities by speed and strength, comparing his results in each category to that of his peers at that position. Speed is exceptionally important, but I'm talking about football speed, not track speed. I've seen a lot of track stars fall on their faces in football, because the sort of speed necessary to succeed on the gridiron is all about anticipation and timing. I look for dominating speed at all positions, asking the question, can a player beat his opponent to a spot? A high school player can gain weight and strength in college, but additional speed is much more difficult to attain.

Strength isn't as important as high school kids believe it is at the high school level. Hundreds of fathers call me every year to tell me that their kid bench presses 350 pounds but doesn't have a great 40-yard dash time. I tell them that it is good for a teenager to be strong, but much more important for a kid that age to have a notable burst of speed as well as flexibility. That father's son could be lifting himself out of a college scholarship.

After reviewing stats and abilities, I then reflect upon my first-person encounters with each prospect. I've seen these kids play, either on the field, in game video, or both. I often wonder how a scout can accurately compare one player against another if that scout hasn't seen both players. Yet that's what other recruiting services do. They have a glut of scouts trying to work together to compile an All-America team. In all my years, I've visited thousands of high schools and never once run into a rival recruiting analyst. Clearly, they've chosen a different path to connect the dots. You decide for yourself which way is best.

When I get down to the final 250 candidates, I spend about two weeks to sort them out. It is an inexact science and a subjective procedure to rank players from 1 through 100. When you get down to the very best players, who is to say who is No. 1 or No. 10? I trust my instincts, compile a final list, and then hope to have a bit of luck in terms of how it all turns out. Injury and changing circumstances can all play havoc with a top 100 list. For example, when evaluating the class of 2006, I spent a lot of time on the top choice at quarterback, watching film of Mitch Mustain and Tim Tebow to determine who was better. I settled on Mustain, purely due to the level of competition he faced in high school.

My job has gotten a little easier over the last six years because I have invited the top 80 players in the country to participate in the U.S. Army All-America Classic. They gather to suit up in San Antonio for seven days in January, where I am able to watch workouts and get progress reports from coaches every day. It is an invaluable aid in making my final evaluations for the year. In 2004, Adrian Peterson and Brian Brohm were the two top players in the country. For most of the year, I rated Brohm ahead of Peterson, but then Peterson was outstanding in San Antonio so I moved him ahead of Brohm. You probably couldn't go wrong with either player, as both figure to be standouts in the NFL.

The U.S. Army Game also gives me an opportunity to evaluate many of the best juniors in the country. The top 500 juniors are invited to San Antonio to participate in the U.S. Army combine. It is the earliest—and the best—of all the combines that are conducted across the country. At least one-third of the prospects I hope to scout show up. They pay their own expenses to work out for two days and test their skills against other blue-chippers.

Still, these extra sneak peaks only ease what is still an immense task. Ultimately, time is the only judge of whether I am right or wrong. No one would be so arrogant as to believe he or she has consistently and accurately picked the No. 1 player in the country. The competition is simply too intense; the risks too gigantic. In recruiting, if you're right five of 10 times, then you are doing a great job. If 50 of my top 100 players in any given class make the NFL or become big-time stars in college, then I'm doing a good job. I'll take a .500 batting average any time.

SECOND QUARTER

6

THE TRIP

I PERSONALLY SEE close to 50 high school games each
year. I also personally interview 95 percent of the top 1,000
prospects, which, if you're good at math, you'll note is about
950 players. To accomplish this, I've had to become very
familiar with America's highways.

Each November, I begin to map out my annual trips, which
begin after Christmas. The reason for those trips is often one
significant game or event; but I make certain to allow enough
time around each event to be able to pack in plenty of
additional scouting. In 2005, for example, I drove to the
Tennessee-Alabama game in Tuscaloosa, Alabama. That game
was the main reason for my trip, but I also scheduled four days
of travel time around that game so I could interview some top
juniors I had heard about in southern Indiana, Kentucky, and
north and central Alabama. In that span, I visited 14 high
schools and talked to nearly 50 kids. Likewise, when I go to
speaking engagements at colleges—I have been invited to
speak about recruiting at Wisconsin every year for the last 16
years, and I also have spoken at Tennessee, Florida, Alabama,
Maryland, Stanford, Kansas, Iowa, Illinois, North Carolina,
and Vanderbilt—I always plan to make it a work trip. I'll see a
high school game on Friday night and do interviews with high

school players in the area before and after my scheduled engagement.

The extreme example of this is the U.S. Army All-America Classic in San Antonio, Texas. For the past six years, I have left after Christmas for that game, a full two weeks early. That allows me just enough time to interview the top 100 players in Texas in addition to players in Missouri, Arkansas, Louisiana, and Oklahoma. It makes for one busy trip, but that's the way I like it.

My total number of trips in one calendar year usually numbers somewhere around 25, and I now travel from coast to coast. I section off the country and plan to meet players at certain spots. For instance, I'll arrange to meet the top players in the Los Angeles area at one location convenient to most of them. I save time by staying on expressways and arranging for groups of players to meet at a McDonald's near an Interstate, or at well-known spot in the city, like Wrigley Field in Chicago or Yankee Stadium in New York. The same goes for the top players in other metropolitan areas such as Detroit, Pittsburgh, Atlanta, Miami, and Boston. I always ask the gathered kids if there is anyone in the area that I may have missed, a player who others think is a potential All-American. So sometimes I'll have to work in a couple extra interviews based on their feedback.

When I return home after the last trip, I bury myself in my office and finish writing my evaluations, cramming as much work as I can into each day to make certain that the writing is completed while the information is still relatively fresh in my mind. After writing the content for my report, I'll edit it, then send it off to the printer. At that point, it's time to start the gathering process all over again for the following year's class, while at the same time keeping my finger on the pulse of the current class. By October, I've received clear reports on the top high school juniors to evaluate. Based upon those reports, I start calling high school coaches to arrange for film to be sent. And the wheels just keep on spinning—there's really no end to the process.

◆　　◆　　◆

Early in my career, when it was time to head out on the road I often suffered panic attacks. I didn't have much money and I certainly didn't have much experience in the field, and all the pressure to succeed sometimes overwhelmed me. I was going into a new field with little guidance or encouragement, not to mention help from college coaches. My funds for my early scouting trips were next to nothing: I could only afford to stay in a cheap motel once every two days, which meant I was sleeping in my car on the off nights. My diet consisted almost exclusively of fast food, because it was cheap and convenient for someone always on the go. I only ate two meals a day—never three. I always skipped breakfast to save money. In the car, I'd snack on bags of candy. I didn't enjoy a sit-down dinner for my first seven years on the road, but now that I can I stop at Cracker Barrels when I can find them. My favorite fast food was White Castle hamburgers. Chicagoans can relate to that. But there are no White Castles in the South, only in the Midwest and in the East. So when I couldn't find a White Castle, I'd settle for McDonald's. I've always been a salad-with-a-donut-chaser kind of guy. You can imagine what people would say today about my diet back then.

I took my first trip in the fall of 1978 to Cincinnati, Detroit, and St. Louis. On that trip, I had to borrow my father's car because mine had broken down. I drove a 1974 Chevrolet Nova, a gas-saver even at a time when gas was cheap. In my first year alone I put 25,000 miles on my car. But I was just beginning—the miles would steadily increase year after year.

I recall driving to Cincinnati on my initial trip to meet coach Pat Mancuso at Princeton at 7:30 in the morning. I slept in the parking lot of a Denny's restaurant the night before. It was so cold that I had to spend some time inside the Denny's just to thaw out. Mancuso showed up with a player I wanted to see, Arnold Franklin, and a few others he wanted to promote.

In that first year, I also made brief trips to Pittsburgh, Indianapolis, and Chattanooga. I planned my trip around leads, sort of a similar approach to a traveling salesman. When I got wind of big-shot prospects—often from a Chicago Catholic newspaper or Bud Wilkinson's magazine or out-of-town newspapers that I read at the newsstand at State and Randolph in Chicago—I would plan trips accordingly.

On the road, I tried to multitask as much as possible. I would stop at radio stations along the way and talk football recruiting, in part to find new leads and in part to advertise my fledgling magazine. While driving, I'd listen to books on tape or talk radio programs. But my main focus remained on seeing as many players as possible, and adding names to my list of contacts. On my early trips, I couldn't afford to call all the high school coaches in advance. So I would simply show up and try to secure a bit of their time. From speaking with one coach, I would find out about other good players in the area, then I would go see them, too. I had to hope that other high school coaches would be as cooperative. At this stage in my career, I relied much more on local newspapers and word of mouth than college coaches for my information on which players were worthy of my attention.

Each year, my trips expanded bit by bit. In the first four years, I couldn't afford to travel beyond the Midwest, except for an occasional drive to Tennessee and Alabama. Pittsburgh, Cincinnati, and Detroit were loaded with good players in the 1970s. So traveling there got me off to a good start. But I was also eager to scout the South more thoroughly. You can trace my love for college football to the South, back to 1971, when I saw my first college game, Alabama versus Southern Mississippi, Johnny Musso and John Hannah versus Ray Guy. I was still in high school at that time, and I quickly became a fan of Bear Bryant. So, when I finally began to earn enough funds to expand my scouting trips—after I had nearly 1,000 subscribers to *Prep Football Report*—I made a point to head south when the weather got cold in Chicago. I traveled to St. Louis, Memphis, Alabama, Mississippi, and Louisiana, criss-crossing the whole Southeast.

In the last four years, my trips have been scheduled in a more manageable order. I travel first to Texas, Louisiana, and Arkansas. My next trip is to Virginia, Maryland, and West Virginia. Then I head to New England, New Jersey, and Eastern and Central Pennsylvania. Next, it's on to Ohio, Michigan, Indiana, and Western Pennsylvania. After that, it's the southeastern swing: I fly into Atlanta, move through Georgia, then Florida, then visit North and South Carolina. I fly home from Durham, North Carolina, and almost as soon as I get home, I start packing for a trip to Wisconsin, where I stop in Milwaukee and Madison. On that same trip, I hit Minnesota, South Dakota, Iowa, Nebraska, Oklahoma, Kansas, and western Missouri. I end with the longest trip of all: the West Coast, which takes two to three weeks and involves 8,000 to 13,000 miles of driving. For that one, I fly into Denver, rent a car, and travel through Colorado, Utah, Arizona, and New Mexico, and then on to California, Oregon, and Washington.

From 1988 to 1994, I made trips out to Hawaii as part of my West Coast tour. I would fly out to cover the Shawn Akina Classic, which pitted six Hawaiian teams against six schools from the Mainland on one Saturday afternoon in late August. While there, I drove around Oahu to interview the best players. Unfortunately, the Classic is no longer being conducted.

Of course, there are some places I miss. I've never been to Monument Valley on the Arizona/Utah border; it always seems to be out of my way. And although I've made it to the South Rim of the Grand Canyon, I've never had enough time to stop and enjoy the view. On my way to Arizona, I've only been able to drive through—and not stop in—Death Valley.

I've never seen a show or gambled during any of my 17 trips to Las Vegas. The only state I have missed altogether is Alaska. But honestly, I don't think I've ever heard of a great football player coming out of Alaska.

In 2005-06, I visited 48 states, drove 55,000 miles and met over 1,200 kids. My first trip, to San Antonio, Texas, began on December 26. My last trip began on June 13. I went to Chicago, Indianapolis, Tuscaloosa, Atlanta, Columbia, Hampton, Richmond, Washington, D.C., Baltimore, Philadelphia, North New Jersey, Pittsburgh, Canton, Akron, and Cleveland—all in six days. The 2006 trip was special for another reason: it was the first time I had *not* received a speeding ticket on one of my trips. I've been ticketed all over the country, for all sorts of reasons. I once got one in Oklahoma for changing lanes too fast.

But between stops, in addition to getting pulled over, I've visited many historic sites and recorded many memories. I've also learned a lot about the kinds of drivers in each state. I think Louisiana has the worst drivers this side of New Jersey. When driving through Louisiana, you always have to be on your toes. Most people drive too fast, with the reckless abandon of someone who has only one day to live. Louisiana drivers come at you from out of nowhere and from all angles. You don't even have to be on an expressway or a local street; you have a tough time avoiding them in parking lots and garages, too. But I've survived it, and along the way I've set some personal records. For example, my longest drive was 1,350 miles in one day, from Tucson to Dallas, a 24-hour adventure I'll never do again. I once drove through a rainstorm from Columbia, South Carolina, to Tallahassee, Florida, that lasted seven hours. And I've driven through tornadoes in Mississippi.

But I'd do it all over again. And I will, beginning this December, for the 28th year in a row.

7

SPREADING THE WORD

PREP FOOTBALL REPORT is the meat and potatoes of my recruiting service. But the bread and butter is the exposure I get from appearing on television and being interviewed regularly on dozens of radio sports talk shows from coast to coast. You can't put a price on such exposure. It gives me an opportunity to promote my magazine and my service, and to update my evaluations and the recruiting status of the top prospects. Football fans can never get enough of it. They want to know who their school is recruiting as well as who is interested in their school.

During the peak recruiting season in January and February, I get over 100 telephone calls a day—and my phone number has been unlisted for eight years. The only people with access are college coaches, sportswriters, family, and friends. Also, I give my number to people at camps; I'm in this business to help people, not just to sell magazines. I often receive 30 messages a day, almost all from sportswriters and radio shows. I get 10 to 15 calls a day from fathers who want me to evaluate their sons to help them to get to college. Blue-chippers call, too. They want to ask how I rank them compared to other outstanding players at their position, how they stack up among the best players in the nation.

Annually, I receive about 500 films in the mail, and I pick up another 700 or so on the road during my trips. Sometimes, parents send film on their son, asking me to give them an honest appraisal. If they've gone to the trouble of mailing a film, I feel obligated to watch it and evaluate it.

I spend five minutes with each film. I can tell in a minute or two if a kid is a legitimate prospect. For example, I only had to watch six or seven plays involving running back Noel Devine of Fort Myers, Florida, one of the leading prospects in the class of 2007, to realize he was a special player. And after one minute of quarterback Jimmy Clausen of Westlake Village, California, I could turn off the projector; he is that good. Most players aren't like that; they're either not big enough or not quick enough. I don't try to discourage them, but I recommend that they look into the Mid-America Conference or Division II schools.

Today, I try to relay the same kind of information to radio listeners and television viewers. I first became affiliated with ESPN back in 1986. I did a recruiting show. ESPN would ask me to come out every now and then, always around signing day. They flew me to their headquarters in Bristol, Connecticut. At the time, it wasn't the giant worldwide corporation that it is now. It had only two buildings—instead of the five it has today—and there was no ESPN2, no ESPN.com or ESPN Classic. But they provided big-time talent for the show. Mike Gottfried was co-host most of the time and Chris Fowler, Gary Danielson, Bill Curry, and Terry Bowden worked with me over what would be a 15-year period.

In 1991, Jim McNeil approached me because he wanted to start a television show on recruiting. He produced a show for the Tallahassee-based Sunshine Network, which covers Florida and other southern states, and now he wanted me to be a part of it. From 1992 to 1999, I did the show once a week, from late November to signing day in February. It was also broadcast in Chicago. Every Monday, I left Chicago at 11 in the morning. There were no direct flights back then, so I would fly from

Chicago through Atlanta or Charlotte, then on to Tallahassee. We taped on Tuesday mornings, so I'd be back in the airport by one in the afternoon.

The show aired on Saturdays. We rated the players and showed them on film. My co-host was Gene Deckerhoff, the voice of the Florida State Seminoles and Tampa Bay Buccaneers. At the end of the year, we did one show at Disney World in Orlando. It was a three-day event, my best time of the year, worth every two-hour flight delay.

I wasn't paid at all for my work, though they did cover my flights, hotel stays, and meals. I knew they had a shoestring budget, so I didn't ask for any money. Besides, it was all about exposure. I knew it would be good for business—and it was. They advertised my magazine on the show and sales went from 3,000 to 4,000 copies in just one year.

Eventually, the show started having trouble attracting sponsors. ESPN and Reebok couldn't agree on expenses. McNeil wasn't making as much money as he thought he could. And honestly, I was getting tired of all the flying. In its last two years, 2000 and 2001, we did only one show, a signing day special in Chicago, where I invited the top 24 players in the country to spend three days in the Windy City. Some of the players who appeared on those last shows were Randy Moss, Charles Woodson, LaVar Arrington, Ron Dayne, Joe Mauer, and Tommie Harris.

In 1998, when I was filing reports for *The Sporting News*, ESPN approached me and said they would double my salary if I worked for them. They wanted me to cover all of their football recruiting, and they wanted me to be available whenever they needed me. I worked for them for the next five years. I never missed an assignment. I was never late. In the fourth year, they started selling subscriptions to their website; my reports and evaluations were included on their paid site, which meant fewer people saw my work.

For eight years, I approached ESPN about doing a different kind of recruiting show. My idea was to interview players the week before signing day, and have them announce then, live on the air, where they were going. If we could have them say where they were going before signing day, not after they had already signed, I was convinced the show could generate huge ratings. But ESPN never wanted to do it; they said they didn't have the budget. Instead, ESPNews wanted me to do a five-minute show on signing day.

So, in December 2004, when I was approached by CSTV, I brought up the same idea with them. CSTV asked me to do a 3-to-11 show on signing day in New York City. They promised I would be on the air for four hours during signing day in 2005. We had a gentlemen's agreement that I would do the show.

Just after New Year's Day, I was working on an ESPN column when I mentioned to a typist that I would be doing a show for CSTV. That information made its way up the ladder, and I eventually learned the bosses were upset. They called me into their offices and said they didn't want me to do CSTV because it was their competitor. At the time, it was a ridiculous argument, like comparing an elephant to a mouse. But ESPN was very much aware that one of the founders of CSTV had founded ESPN Classic.

I wasn't into the squabble. I just wanted to do a television show. I argued that I had no TV contract with ESPN and that ESPN didn't have any plans to put a Tom Lemming show on the air. They countered with the argument that they just didn't want me working for CSTV. In the end, I decided to honor my commitment to CSTV. A couple of days before the signing day, ESPNews called me. They wanted me to do reports for them. I said I could do it, but that I would have to work around my CSTV show. It seemed like one division of ESPN didn't talk to another division. They said they wouldn't look favorably upon it.

I haven't heard from ESPN since. They decided to have Scout Inc. do their recruiting, which is fine with me because I'm very happy at CSTV. I do a column and top 100 ratings and evaluations for CSTV.com, and I have my own show, *Tom Lemming's Generation Next*, a weekly program that airs from late August until signing day in February. The brainchild of Tim Pernetti, a former football player at Rutgers and current CSTV program director, the show is 30 minutes long and taped in New York and Chicago. My co-host, Greg Amsinger, and I, along with our producer, Steve Hauser, discuss current news items on recruiting, rate players by position, and attract most of the major coaches and players as guests. Some of my guests have been Texas' Mack Brown, Notre Dame's Charlie Weis, Michigan's Lloyd Carr, and Florida's Urban Meyer. We're proud of our show; there is nothing else like it around the country.

◆　　◆　　◆

I once had to change my phone number after it was listed on a university's Internet site in January 2005. They listed it to get even with me for what they perceived as a slap in the face to their program. I even got a death threat. Thankfully, in the real world, football recruiting is entertainment, not a life-or-death situation as some fans make it out to be.

The big explosion in recruiting-as-entertainment occurred in the mid-1980s. Everybody started to follow it more. To a lot of college football fans, signing day in February was as festive as the Fourth of July and as important as their wedding anniversary. People would call me at all hours of the day and night to get updates. They even knocked on my front door. While looking through my front window, one person asked, "Can you tell me what Iowa is doing?" In those days, few players made early commitments, so it wasn't until signing day itself that we would know for sure who'd go where. For some, it was as suspenseful as an Alfred Hitchcock movie.

USA Today, the first national newspaper, printed recruiting lists the day after signing day. Recruiting was a popular topic of conversation on radio sports talk shows, particularly in small college towns. I recall doing over 100 radio shows in January and February, including 50,000-watt stations in Chicago, Detroit, Cincinnati, Des Moines, and New Orleans.

In the 1990s, however, the Internet came into being and recruiting changed forever. I wasn't aware of it because I didn't have a computer. But it was here to stay and it made an enormous impact on recruiting. The Internet emerged as an ultimate source of information; the NCAA was able to post its rules, which meant there was no excuse for playing dumb when it came to what was and wasn't allowed in recruiting. And suddenly, every Division I college had its own website. Recruiting websites also sprung up all over the Web. Van Coleman, one of the leading basketball analysts in the country, once said that a lot of the people purporting to be recruiting evaluators are in reality only recruiting reporters, people without an educated eye who over-evaluate prospects. I happen to agree with that statement.

I'm not an Internet guy. Most websites make the majority of their revenue from kids and parents who subscribe to their service. In turn, those players are treated like rock stars, getting a lot of coverage even if they aren't Division I prospects. Some websites hoodwink prospects into thinking they have more potential than they actually do, which persuades them to pay subscription or premium fees. Along the way, accuracy often gets lost. Websites compete with each other by trying to prolong the recruitment process and by being the first with a story—the first to gain new information about a player's commitment.

The Internet can at times feel like a faceless, anonymous technology that manufactures a lot of negative, inaccurate, and misleading information. The recruiting business in general can be exceptionally negative and aggressive, and the Internet is a place where a lot of that negativity rises up. I'm one of the few recruiters left who isn't connected to one of the big websites, and I cherish my individuality.

A good aspect of the Internet's prominence in recruiting is the information it provides, and the public availability of that information. No longer is there a code of silence among colleges and recruiters. Every prospect knows where every top player is going. But misinformation on the Internet is rampant. Fans have become part of the process by printing rumors and inaccurate reports. A lot of negative recruiting is going on. Anonymous contributors can post virtually anything they choose, though not always without repercussions.

On a Chicago-based website, a subscriber in a chat room said that Santino Panico, an All-Chicago Area football player from Libertyville, had failed a drug test at Nebraska and wouldn't play as a freshman. Panico doesn't even drink soda— let alone take drugs—and he started at Nebraska as a punt returner. Panico's father, Anthony, learned about the story and called the website owner, who said he couldn't reveal the name of the poster. Panico's lawyer called Rivals, the website's owner, and threatened to sue if the name wasn't revealed. He eventually got the name.

Some players have told me that they intentionally feed false information to Internet people. Why do they do it? Just for fun, they say. They'll tell one site that a particular school is their favorite, but then tell another site that a different school is their favorite. I'm convinced that a majority of players take the content of the Internet with a grain of salt—at least, I hope that's the case.

The Internet does give instant information on recruiting to die-hard football fans. And fans love it. Websites write weekly stories that detail each campus visit, almost every phone call between coaches and prospects. But most college football fans don't follow the process throughout the year: most don't get caught up in the artificial hype. They realize that what really matters is the day a player makes his commitment.

But the Internet supports another kind of fan—those who live their lives through their team's wins and losses and recruiting successes, or lack thereof, and their passion for all of this sometimes borders on lunacy.

Of course, the Internet has affected my business. I once sold 4,000 magazines annually. Now I sell 3,000. I still have a 900-number, which was very profitable in January and February in the 1990s. I used to get several hundreds of calls a day during the week before signing day. Now I get only 200. I might be the only 900-number still out there. But like I said, I'm proud of my individuality, so if I'm the only 900 number left, that's only more to be proud of.

8

RECRUITING—THE SECOND SEASON

DICK BUTKUS NEVER FORGOT what he referred to as the "salesmanship" of Illinois head coach Pete Elliott and assistant coach Bill Taylor when he went through the recruiting process in 1960. When he visited Notre Dame, his first choice, he was turned off when he asked school officials if he could get married before he graduated and was informed that he could not. Later, when he visited Illinois, he asked the same question of Elliott and Taylor. "Yes, by all means," they told him. They even showed Butkus and his future wife, Helen, where they would live and offered to assist Helen in her job search.

In his autobiography, *Butkus: Flesh and Blood, How I Played the Game*, after an Indiana alum tried to persuade him to renege on his commitment to Illinois by offering him a new Corvette, Butkus said, "This was 1960, and although few of us knew it then, the American code of ethics was already undergoing a heavy rewrite, and in the years to come, I would meet more men who preferred to operate in the dark."

Butkus said in all his school visits, he didn't receive a single under-the-table offer from a coach. That's the way it was in the 1960s; coaches didn't get involved in the exchanges, but they were well aware of the alumni who did. I saw an extraordinary number of alumni who were involved in the recruiting process. The alumni had the blessing of the coaches. But the coaches kept their hands off.

In the 1970s, college coaches relied on alumni to recommend prospects. Alumni scouted players in their areas and checked out all-star teams in their local newspapers. Alumni would initially meet with players and their parents, take them out to dinner, and give them the royal treatment. They'd feel out a prospect, trying to determine if the player— or his parents—seemed willing to take a handout: money under the table, a car, a job he doesn't have to work at. If so, the alumni would take care of everything. I recall some Wisconsin alumni took a recruit from Georgia on a boat and didn't bring him back until after signing day. The prospect wanted to attend Wisconsin, but those alumni wanted to make sure that no southern school could influence him at the last minute.

In my view, half the schools in the country were cheating in the late 1970s, some minor, some major. Everyone wanted to get a step ahead of the competition. And, because the NCAA wasn't doing a very good job of policing the recruiting process, they usually got away with it. There was so much cheating, so many excesses, that the NCAA finally was forced to crack down in the 1970s and 1980s.

Part of the problem was that, in the 1950s and 1960s, there was no such thing as a recruiting coordinator in college football. The title didn't exist. Each coach recruited mainly from his own area. But aside from the unofficial influence of alumni, there was no one person in charge of recruiting, no one to pin names on a board.

All of that began to change in the 1970s. The first person to make a name for himself as a recruiting coordinator was Jerry Pettibone at Oklahoma under Barry Switzer. That was the first time I even heard the term recruiting coordinator. There were a lot of media interviews, which helped Pettibone and Switzer establish themselves as recruiters, not just coaches. Switzer and Pettibone worked hand in hand; they were superb at getting the media involved with stories about top prospects and letting recruits know how good they were. In those days, it was very important for coaches to have contacts with sportswriters and high school coaches. A recruiter needed a great work ethic and an even better personality if he was going to find and persuade players to come to his school. There were a lot of sleepers at that time—farm boys from Oklahoma, shrimpers from Louisiana, clam-shuckers from Massachusetts—and it took a lot of resources and work to find them. Switzer and Pettibone used the media better than anyone had ever done before, eventually becoming one of the most successful recruiting duos in history.

In his recruiting efforts, Switzer often relaxed and became "one of the guys." He acted, talked, and joked like the players he was recruiting. Once, Switzer slept on a couch in Alvin Ross' house in Aurora, Illinois, so that he'd be there to sign him before other schools were allowed in the house. Ross, a running back, was one of the top prospects in the Chicago area in 1980, and no one knew whether he would sign with Oklahoma or Illinois. Head coaches were waiting at Ross' house at eight in the morning on signing day. When they knocked on the door, Switzer opened it. He walked out with Ross' signature. That's the kind of dedication Switzer was willing to make in his dual role as coach and recruiting coordinator.

Pettibone was a different yet equally effective breed of recruiter. He worked hard and called players, focusing on personal contact. Very charming and friendly, like Switzer, he made sure players knew that Oklahoma wanted them, not that they should feel honored to be recruited by a college. Pettibone eventually became head coach at Northern Illinois, and later, at Oregon State.

Switzer and Pettibone were miles ahead of their rivals when it came to racially integrating college football—they integrated their program in the 1970s. But when it came to recruiting African-American athletes, Michigan State coach

Duffy Daugherty revolutionized the process in the 1960s. He was the first of the big-name recruiters, the one who wrote the book, so to speak. And he was the first to step into an area of controversy where others were reluctant to tread. Daugherty had brought in many of the black athletes playing in Northern schools. But he also brought in players from Hawaii and from the Deep South. He brought in Bubba Smith from Texas and George Webster from South Carolina. He went where Southeast Conference coaches wouldn't go: into the homes of great African-American athletes in the South.

Daugherty followed Biggie Munn and made Michigan State a national power for a number of years. Other coaches began to notice what Daugherty was doing, including John McKay at USC, and Bear Bryant at Alabama. Bryant once said that the performance of Sam Cunningham, an African-American tailback at USC, against Alabama at Legion Field in Birmingham, did more for integration in the South than anything else he could think of.

Ohio State's Woody Hayes also was cultivating new ground. He was the first big name to go into players' homes and spend a lot of time on the road seeing them. Other big-name coaches, such as Bear Bryant, Notre Dame's Ara Parseghian, and Nebraska's Bob Devaney, were reluctant to visit players in their homes because they believed things shouldn't be done that way. Prospects should come to them, they thought. Assistant coaches went after kids, not head coaches. But Hayes did a lot to change that mentality.

Once the position of "Recruiting Coordinator" came into existence, it didn't take long for most programs to pick up on it. In the 1970s, recruiting coordinators began springing up everywhere, competing for bragging rights about incoming classes on signing day. Pettibone went to Nebraska, Oklahoma's archrival, becoming their recruiting coordinator.

Then others began to surface—Artie Gigantino at USC, Fran Ganther at Penn State, Fritz Seyferth at Michigan, Brian Boulac at Notre Dame, just to name a few.

Later, in 1985, Vinny Cerrato took over at Notre Dame. He took the job to another level. He was very innovative, so much so that the NCAA had to adopt new rules to put everyone on a level playing field. In those days, a coach could go on the road in the spring and fall. Cerrato, a coach in name only, was on the road all the time, scouting football recruits and watching them play. He was the only college coach who spent more time on the road than on campus, and that gave Notre Dame a huge advantage in making evaluations.

Cerrato was in his 20s at the time, and he could relate to teenagers. He was one of the first recruiters to begin the practice of calling players via cell phones from the field during a college game. Cerrato had the idea of recruiting players based on athletic ability more than production. He took into account if a prospect could play basketball well; if he could jump and run, he could play other positions on the football team. He also had a knack for persuading recruits to be quiet about their commitment for months. No one knew whom the school had. Notre Dame brought out all of their signees at the end of the recruiting period. There might be seven or eight future NFL running backs on the roster at one time, but the players wouldn't know who else was on the list until they'd already committed to Notre Dame. So coach Lou Holtz could stockpile talent. Other schools have since learned to copy the practice, but Cerrato brought it into existence.

Until Cerrato's arrival, Notre Dame had been relying mainly on its tradition to sell recruits on its program. But athletes wanted more than tradition in their college experience. Cerrato sold Notre Dame's education prowess, as well as its good record when it came to sending former students to the NFL. In fact, Cerrato became so good at his job that rival schools complained about his effectiveness and Notre Dame's recruiting advantage. In response, the NCAA made a point to reduce the number of assistants from 10 to nine, and declared that all of them had to be coaches on the field. They couldn't travel carte blanche ala Cerrato anymore.

In the past 30 years of Notre Dame football, Cerrato was the second most important, just after Holtz. But he receives very little recognition. He was instrumental in all of the great athletes coming to Notre Dame. Between 1985 and 1992, over 70 of them went on to play in the NFL, more than any other college team. From a recruiting standpoint, he brought Notre Dame into the modern era. The day he left South Bend, in the spring of 1992, to go to the San Francisco 49ers as the player development coordinator, it sent Notre Dame into a downward spiral that it didn't recover from for 13 years. That just goes to show you how much a recruiting coordinator influences their team.

◆ ◆ ◆

What is the job of today's recruiting coordinators? A coordinator must be personable. He must have a good work ethic, must be innovative. Coordinators have to stay on top of everything. But most of all, they must have great evaluating skills.

Organization is becoming more important than ever before. There are so many prospects out there, and you have to keep track of them. A coordinator at Michigan—or Texas, or any big-time school—will receive 2,000 tapes in the mail. Many of them won't even be solicited. But as a good coordinator, you can't afford not to look at all of them, for fear you will miss the next Dick Butkus or John Elway. Last year, I was most impressed with the organization and work of Kent McLeod, the director of football operations at Ole Miss. He works for Ed Orgeron, who came from USC, where he was the Trojans' best recruiter. He is doing a masterful job of resurrecting a program that was once a national power under Johnny Vaught.

McLeod is the wave of the future when it comes to the recruiter's role. He dedicates more working hours to recruiting than most schools. He conducts one recruiting meeting daily with the staff. McLeod's job is organizational in nature, quickly obtaining tape and organizing assistants to evaluate it as promptly as possible. It is very important for second- or third-tier schools like Ole Miss—which isn't in a class with Florida or Georgia in the SEC—to work more quickly. The national college football powerhouses do a lot of their recruiting on a local level: Miami signs a lot of players from south Florida, then spot recruits the top 200 in the nation. USC does the same thing in southern California, Ohio State in Ohio, Texas in Texas, and so on. They are so successful in their own areas that they only have to recruit a few super players nationally. Notre Dame, Nebraska, and Tennessee must go out of state because there are so few stars locally; they're the only members of the Super Sixteen that are forced to go out of their immediate areas and recruit nationally. Smaller programs have it even worse when it comes to finding talent outside their local radius. Schools like Ole Miss need to get films of juniors sooner than their more powerful rivals, and to get as many films as possible. That's how McLeod has managed to do so well when it comes to recruiting.

When I was at Ole Miss, McLeod had hundreds of films in his library. In October and November, he already had a long list of promising juniors—at that time of year, most schools are still looking at seniors. McLeod has a staff of student workers to help break down films. Their job also involves sending mailings to every high school in the nation, inquiring if they have any Division I players.

McLeod and his staff are doing what needs to be done when it comes to their program, coming at it with the same attitude as a Cerrato or a Pettibone. And just like in its first days, the role of the recruiting coordinator continues to change shape.

9

THE RULES: THEN, NOW, AND TOMORROW

TWENTY YEARS AGO, head coaches could be in a recruit's home on signing day. It was a great advantage, especially with the most sought-after players. Coaches also used to be able to visit a recruit's home on three occasions, and energetic coaches took advantage of that number, making all three allowed visits. But the NCAA changed the rules, forbidding coaches from being in a player's home on signing day and limiting a head coach to only one home visit.

The NCAA also dramatically reduced the amount of time coaches are allowed to spend on the road, as well as the number of phone calls they can make to recruits. Now they can go on the road only in May, December, and January. They can make only one phone call in May, and another one between signing day in February to September 1. In September, October, and November, they can call no more than once a week. Once December and January roll around, they can make calls to players daily.

The NCAA updates its rules to keep up with the creative ways some programs try to bend them. The NCAA recently legislated against text messaging. One mother of a Georgia recruit complained that she had a monthly phone bill over $200, with most of the cost coming from coaches' text messages.

After the NCAA forced every coach to be on the field, eliminating the "coaches in name only," schools appointed another person to serve as a director of operations. That meant each school had one position coach designated as recruiting coordinator in addition to a director of operations, who wasn't a coach, running the program; the colleges were trying to sneak around the rules. But the NCAA picked up on their strategy, so it ruled that the director of operations couldn't watch film or call prospects.

It happens on the smallest of scales. When I began traveling around the country to meet and evaluate high school athletes, I noted that colleges were able to feed recruits every time they stepped on the campus. That practice stopped when college officials realized that coaches at high schools near college campuses used the policy as a lunch program for their players. Now students must pay for their own food, lodging, and transportation during any unofficial visit.

But there are areas, when it comes to recruiting, that the NCAA sometimes seems to forget. Nationally, there are about 25 schools that will do whatever it takes to get great players. They have systems in place where players accept payoffs from alumni and others who have been involved in the programs for years. In these cases, the coaches are aware of what is going on but their hands are clean. By this point, it is too difficult for the administration to control alumni associations that have gotten too involved in football. Almost every college has rich alumni who live their lives vicariously through the football program, and because of all the money they donate, schools are reluctant to get rid of them.

Alumni or alumni groups can be powerful. In addition to under-the-table payoffs, powerful alumni sometimes offer to help to get a recruit's family member out of jail or providing them with a job, sometimes even a home. There have been many stories of rich alumni flying recruits to schools in private jets. There were cases of underage drinking, recruits being taken to strip joints and off-campus parties. At one college, someone paid for call girls for recruits.

Unfortunately, these kinds of temptations play a part in the college choice a recruit eventually makes. Some kids say they picked schools strictly on the basis of which ones were the best party schools. But the temptations aren't limited to the players: For years, when I was driving through Memphis, I heard rumors about an Alabama alum who was paying off high school coaches to persuade them to send their players to Alabama. The rumor proved to be true when he was caught. I've been privy to stories about college coaches having love affairs with a player's mother in order to influence her son to attend a certain school.

Some scandals only come to light after newspapers publish front-page stories, or after parents see their sons being arrested on the ten o'clock news. One case was Willie Williams of Miami, Florida, one of the nation's leading prospects a few years ago. He agreed to write a recruiting diary for *The Miami Herald*. Williams was arrested during his official visit to the Florida campus for bad behavior. At that time, it was discovered he had previous arrests. It was shocking news to people who couldn't understand why someone with his tainted background was being treated like royalty.

The Willie Williams case made the public aware of what a lot of us in the recruitment industry had known for years: official campus visits were sometimes nothing but 48 hours of party time. Only in the wake of such bad publicity does the NCAA feel forced to take action.

In addition to stepping up when it comes to recruiting violations, the NCAA must do a better job of monitoring the academic standing of incoming athletes. Colleges welcome a lot of players who have trouble reading and writing in high school because they are blue-chip athletes. The NCAA does a decent job of keeping up with outright crimes and rules violations, but, in my opinion, their biggest failure is their reluctance to stand up and declare that some players just aren't qualified to be in college.

Through my work ranking players, I see a lot of GPAs, test scores, and transcripts, so I know there are an alarming number of students who don't yet belong in college. I know that many of them need junior college degrees before they are academically ready to go to a four-year school. Over the years, I'd say I've seen over 1,000 kids who should have gone to junior colleges, but because of their enormous talent, they were admitted to four-year schools, schools they were not academically equipped to attend.

A lot of these players have been getting free passes for years; it's a practice that existed long before I started evaluating players. It usually begins in high school: because of a player's athletic ability, schools sometimes go easy when it comes to academics so that the student will be eligible to compete in sports. Coaches and school administrations sometimes put pressure on teachers, reminding them that they don't want to be accused of holding a student back, thus ruining a potential NFL or NBA career. As far as I know, the NCAA does not investigate big jumps in grade point averages in high school from junior to senior years, so the question lingers: is the athlete really doing the work, or are teachers giving him grades to make him eligible for a college scholarship?

College admission boards regularly make exceptions for athletes they really want, admitting them even if their GPAs or test scores don't reach that particular school's minimum. College admissions personnel claim, correctly, that some students don't test well but are capable of doing college work. They use the same argument for athletes with sub par grades. It makes sense that a high school athlete who must go to practice, attend team meetings and weight-training sessions, and play in games will not have the same amount of time to study as a non-athlete, and therefore bend the standards when it comes to admissions. But the student will have similar—if not, more intense—demands on his time once enrolled and playing college ball, so a school can't reasonably expect their grades to magically improve and meet their academic standards. The point is this: there are a lot of players going to schools that, according to their grades and test scores, they just don't deserve to attend.

Some colleges manage to get academically unqualified students admitted by enrolling them in night school and summer bridge programs. Schools find ways around the rules to get great players into school, using methods that aren't offered to non-athlete students. Then, once that player gets to college, counselors set up their course schedules and arrange for tutoring, the main goal being not their academic success, but instead keeping them eligible to play football. It's rumored that at some schools, as long as a player attends class and doesn't get into trouble, they'll retain their eligibility. I once heard of a student who didn't attend class at all for an entire semester but was allowed to play in a New Year's bowl game. Following his performance, he declared for the NFL draft. It's clear his academic success wasn't important to him, either.

The private schools—Duke, Notre Dame, and Northwestern, just to name a few—run the cleanest ships when it comes to college sports because coaches are taken out of the equation during the admissions process. The dean of admissions—not the coach—has the final say regarding who is and who isn't accepted. At some state schools, a powerful coach can get most players accepted, no matter how low their grades or test scores. But at private schools, the admissions office has more control. At those institutions, no coach is powerful enough to force the head of admissions to back off. Consequently, the coaches at private schools consistently have to reject great players who want to enroll: Carson Palmer wasn't admitted to Notre Dame; Barry Sanders was turned down by Northwestern; Reggie Bush was rejected by Stanford. But even these schools sometimes make exceptions. Even Stanford will drastically lower its standards when it comes to test scores, admitting football players with scores as low as 1,100—a number far below that of their typical applicants.

In the end, of course, it's all about winning, which is why schools are willing to accept players who read at a fourth- or fifth-grade level. Winning programs make money for the school by filling huge stadiums and keeping rich alumni happy. Winning teams sell more merchandise, and profits help pay the big salaries demanded by most coaches. Money pours into college football at such an extraordinary rate that nobody wants to rock the boat—not even the NCAA. The case of offensive lineman Michael Oher is a recent example. Oher has been touted as a future NFL star and was even the subject of *New York Times* writer Michael Lewis' acclaimed book *The Blind Side*. In high school, Oher had a 1.6 grade-point average (on a 4.0 scale) but somehow qualified for Ole Miss. Oher took night courses through the mail, and the grades from those replaced his F's with A's. By doing this, he managed to avoid the wrath of an NCAA investigation. What the Michael Oher case shows is that if you're good enough, college coaches will find a way to get you into school. No matter what the NCAA wants to do, the power schools will always be a step ahead of them.

What personally bothers me is the attitude of some coaches: they act as if they're helping a student by providing a college education (an education, mind you, that he is not prepared to handle), when all they actually care about is having a winning football program. If a young man weren't a difference-maker, a potential All-American, some coaches wouldn't give a damn. In fact, few students who are thought of as vital to team success ever become ineligible while in college, but those who don't turn out to be as good as a coach had hoped sometimes find themselves flunking out. All a coach needs to do to get rid of a player he doesn't want anymore is expose a player's poor academic standing.

For the benefit of the student athletes and their education, the NCAA also needs to address the area of bogus academics once students reach a college campus. The NCAA doesn't currently look into how many players are intensely tutored just so they maintain the required GPA to be eligible for four years. The numbers don't prevent this kind of vigilance: with 85 scholarship players at 117 Division I schools, the NCAA should be able to monitor the issue—if it wanted to.

Although the NCAA does set academic standards, it should also put in place rules regarding how players achieve those standards. It needs to look into what courses athletes enroll in. It needs to see that a student is pursuing a legitimate, worthwhile degree. The NCAA needs to be sure that a player's GPA hasn't been padded by the school, that he isn't being pushed along by the system with a wink and a nod. If a player has a 1.5 grade point average (on a 4.0 scale) and improves to a 2.5 in just one semester, a red flag should go up and an investigation should be conducted to make sure that improvement was legitimately achieved.

But the NCAA is reluctant to fix things, although they must know a lot of what's really going on. To me, the NCAA seems to attack the peripheral, the incidents that aren't really of a serious nature. But I've spent a lot of time thinking about simple ways they could fix the recruiting process and eliminate the kinds of issues players face once they enroll at a college.

First off, if I were the imaginary NCAA czar in charge of recruiting, I would pay the players a standard monthly stipend of $500 while on campus, September through May, to provide for incidentals. Athletes aren't allowed to work, but like all college students, they need spending money for necessities that aren't provided by scholarships—and it's safer—and fairer—for this money to come from the NCAA in a regulated form than from rich alumni, who aren't always subject to rules. Five hundred dollars isn't too much to ask when you consider that athletes bring in millions of dollars for the school.

Secondly, I would allow coaches to go back on the road most of the year to evaluate high school or junior college players, as they used to do in the 1980s. The NCAA put a stop to that practice because other coaches complained that highly ambitious coaches, like UCLA's Bill Rees and Notre Dame's Vinny Cerrato, had a big advantage and were on the road too much. But the extra time would make for a less cutthroat recruitment period.

I'd make several other changes as well. If the NCAA is truly interested in putting a stop to illegal recruiting and cheating of any kind, it should beef up its investigative staff to police the rules. They don't seem to have enough manpower to check out rumors or reports of rules violations. And I would make the NCAA get more serious about academics by installing an academic enforcement officer. When I am gathering data about athletes for my magazine—statistics, honors, grades—I am always baffled because I receive different academic information than what is eventually given to the media when they sign. An academic enforcement officer could look into these discrepancies. Once the recruitment period is over and a player is enrolled in classes, I would look into the kinds of courses that football player is taking to make sure he is enrolled in a curriculum that would allow him to progress toward a worthwhile degree.

Another change that could make the recruitment process more pleasant came to me from my old friend, Bob Chmiel, who was recruiting coordinator at Northern Illinois, Northwestern, Michigan, and Notre Dame. His idea is to set aside one month, June or July, and designate it a complete dead period for recruiting: a time when no one talks to anybody—no letters, no text messaging, no phone calls. That way, coaches could lead normal lives with their families, confident that no one was getting the edge on them. And players could just be worry-free kids for at least part of their summer. A lot of college coaches choose to go to the NFL because they get tired of recruiting, and a month-long break—enforced by the NCAA—might help reduce the number of coaches who leave college football for that reason.

I'd make one final, but significant, change: I wouldn't allow colleges to offer any scholarships until September 1 of a player's senior year. That rule would give colleges more time to evaluate players, so they'd make fewer mistakes. It would also go a long way towards deflating player egos, and it would cut down the number of times recruiting analysts called players. But I understand a rule like this won't help everyone; early scholarship offers are the main recruiting tool for smaller or weaker football schools, and they need to be able to contact players and make offers before those students hit the radars of bigger and more established programs.

The tactic of offering early scholarships began at Penn Sate in 1993. The year before, Joe Paterno lost the top 10 players in Pennsylvania. So he ordered his staff to go out and evaluate all the top kids in the East earlier than anyone else and offered those students scholarships when they were just juniors. It had never been done before to that great an extent. At first, there was mass confusion in the college football world; other schools didn't know how to react to Paterno's strategy. They didn't know if they should evaluate students quicker and make offers sooner because not doing so meant possibly losing a prospect to Penn State. But if they spent more time evaluating and didn't offer scholarships until they found the right players, they would make fewer mistakes and know more about the players they were signing. Their choice is now history: after that year, a majority of schools across the country began to offer scholarships to juniors.

Almost every coach I've talked to has said he would like to go back to the old ways and wait until players were seniors before offering scholarships. But all of them felt compelled to offer early and not risk losing a blue-chip prospect. Today, all of the top 200 players have been offered scholarships by the end of June; most offers are made before he steps on the field as a senior. A player's senior year has been largely eliminated from the recruiting equation, meaning one full year of evaluating has been lost. NFL coaches say they need every minute possible to evaluate players. But colleges don't have that luxury. They don't have time to see how a 16- or 17-year-old progresses physically and mentally. They have to take gambles on players they think will be good rather than be certain. Delaying scholarship offers until a player's senior year would get that time back, letting schools make better choices because there's more time to evaluate them.

Instead of considering big changes in the process, the NCAA tends to focus on small, almost unimportant issues. For years, I have arranged for high school players to meet me on college campuses for interviews. I always choose a picturesque spot to take photo. In 2001, when I took photos with players at the University of Virginia, other schools expressed displeasure. So the Atlantic Coast Conference adopted what some coaches amusingly called the "Tom Lemming Rule": if recruits have a picture taken on a campus, they can't meet with the coaches that day. Instead, they must come back the next day. The NCAA is concerned that the publicity that comes with a photo like that helps only one school, despite the fact that I've taken pictures with prospects at almost every one of 117 Division I schools. A rule like that, in the face of so many other glaring problems, is just silly.

10

U.S. ARMY GAME

FOR 20 YEARS, while I was working for the world's largest sports network, I told programming executives that interest in high school football was exploding all over the country. I said they should televise an All-America high school all-star game and a signing show on the Sunday before national signing day in February. I was convinced the two events would be ratings winners and I told them so. But throughout the 1980s and '90s, ESPN told me that it wouldn't fly. Now, ESPN is trying to do it. And so is everybody else.

Today, there are three national all-star games. NBC picked up the U.S. Army game when ESPN dropped the ball, and that game has become the biggest and most important of the three. Then ESPN snagged the new East-West game in Orlando, Florida. It is sponsored by MSL, which runs combines. And Rivals, the scouting service, joined the Offense-Defense game in Fort Lauderdale, Florida. I predict that in the next year or two, CBS or ABC will televise their own all-star games to compete against NBC's U.S. Army game. That's how big high school football is getting. But it took a while for the big networks to put all the pieces of the puzzle together. And if it wasn't for the U.S. Army, it might never have happened.

Seven years ago, Richard McGuinness, the president of SportsLink, Inc., founded the U.S. Army All-American Football Classic. It wasn't a very memorable debut, however. After McGuinness called and asked me to select the team, I circled the names of 60 players in my magazine that I thought should play in the inaugural game in Dallas. It was scheduled to be televised by the Fox network.

But a majority of the players didn't accept their invitations to participate. I remember calling Joe Mauer, a quarterback from St. Paul, Minnesota—the same Joe Mauer of the Minnesota Twins and the leading hitter in the American League in 2006—who was the top-rated high school football player in the nation, and he said he didn't want to play. Back then, players were being discouraged from participating in all-star games. Coaches warned them they could get hurt, which could ruin their college or professional careers.

But McGuinness and SportsLink, based in Hackettstown, New Jersey, were determined to make their game a success. They didn't want to return to Dallas, however. The city did little to promote it, and Dallas just didn't embrace the game. McGinnis had to find it a new home. Then the U.S. Army came to the rescue. Just when McGuinness and others were beginning to think their first all-star game would be their last, the U.S. Army announced it would sponsor the event. They saw it as a recruiting bonanza, a vehicle to get 17- and 18-year-olds to join the Army, and they provided limitless funding. They wanted the very best game and wanted everything connected with the event to be just as spectacular. They arranged for players and coaches to stay at the Westin, one of San Antonio's finest hotels. That generated a lot of excitement, and the game was saved.

In 2001, McGuinness asked me to fly to San Antonio, Texas, to participate in a press conference on the 50-yard-line of the Alamo Bowl, where the U.S. Army made their sponsorship official. Unlike Dallas, San Antonio was small enough to embrace the game but big enough to attract a lot of people. In fact, I think it's the best city in the country for the game because the weather is always good for outdoor practices and it's a great tourist town.

That year, McGuinness asked me to take a more active role in the selection process; he wanted me to choose both teams. I drew up a list of 76 candidates and 45 agreed to participate. As was the case in 2000, some were scared to play because they worried they might get hurt and damage their careers. But I persuaded Vince Young and Maurice Clarett, two of the nation's leading players, to participate in the game, which was televised by ESPN2. But the game, which wasn't promoted very well, attracted only lukewarm ratings. Still, the U.S. Army stuck by it and did a great job of stabilizing it. In 2003, the game took off big-time when NBC replaced ESPN as the television outlet.

The U.S. Army, though, didn't want just a game; they wanted a weeklong festival. They wanted a combine to attract younger kids. They also wanted to conduct a cheerleading contest and military maneuvers. As added attractions, the Army asked retired Brig. Gen. Pete Dawkins, a former Heisman Trophy winner, to be present at the event. And Ken Hall of Sugar Land, Texas, a local hero and a 1953 high school graduate who once held 17 national offensive records, annually presents the most valuable player award. As if that weren't enough, the Army also invites such NFL Hall of Fame players as Jim Brown, Barry Sanders, and Anthony Muñoz to speak to the players. The combine is the best in the country. They invite 500 juniors to come to the game and spend three days in San Antonio, going through drills and listening to lectures and getting great exposure. The event draws the best players and the best teachers, and it offers the best facilities.

The 2005 combine was best of all. Almost every great quarterback in the country attended the event—Tim Tebow, Mitch Mustain, Matt Stafford, Jevan Snead, Josh Freeman, Pat Devlin, and Demetrius Jones. The best players in the camp were offensive lineman Andre Smith, who committed to

Alabama, and wide receiver Percy Harvin, who went to Florida. They were standouts in last year's all-star game.

For me, the event is a great time to make evaluations. I have an opportunity to observe most of the best young prospects in the country and to interview them before anyone else knows who they are. Three or four months after the Army game, after they've attended other combines and summer camps, they will be big names from coast to coast, and other recruiting analysts and college recruiters will jump on them in April and May. But I'm able to watch them run the 40 and go through various drills, then talk to them ahead of everyone else, and before some of them get big heads. The event showcases what kind of athletes and competitors they are, and it gets me off to a good start each year.

Eventually, I approached McGuinness with the idea of having some of the top players make their college announcements during the game. McGuinness loved the idea. A year in advance, I talked to Curtis Leak, the father of Chris Leak, who figured to be the national player of the year, and asked if Chris would complete his recruiting process before game day and announce during halftime. Curtis agreed. The following year, Chris announced for Florida and started the ball rolling. Reggie Bush and Lendale White asked if they could make their commitments during the game. NBC loved the idea so much that they said they wanted 20 players to announce every year.

Sometimes it works and sometimes it doesn't. Last year, Jai Eugene announced for Michigan during the game. A week later, he switched to LSU. And Michael Goodson, one of the nation's premier running backs, was going to announce for USC. But a few minutes earlier, Emmanuel Moody chose USC. So Goodson postponed his announcement. Later, he picked Texas A&M. The most talked-about announcements were in 2004, when five All-Americans, including four from the Chicago area, committed to Iowa. It was one of the biggest moments in the history of Iowa recruiting. After the game,

Iowa fans, who had made the long trip to celebrate the moment, had a big barbecue outside the stadium.

In my mind, the players announcing their school choices during the game is what put it over the top. Fans watched to see where the top players were going to go, hoping their favorite school would land one of the best players in the nation. Producers of the show added to the suspense by having the player choose one team's cap from three or four laid out in front of him. It was great entertainment—strictly show business.

I was responsible for choosing the teams from 2001 to 2005. In 2005, Rivals.com approached Rich McGuinness—despite my longtime relationship with him and the Army game—and offered him $100,000 to replace me and let them pick the players. McGuinness said no, and in a true expression of loyalty, he even played me the tape of their telephone conversation.

In 2006, Scout.com joined the party, but I still play a major role in the selection process and I can honestly say I haven't had a problem with the way it is handled today. Every player that I've felt should be invited to play in the game has been selected. Scout.com and I have been on the same page for the last two years. I handpick the 80 participants with help from Scout.com, which pays to be part of the selection process, and Zach Morolda of SportsLink, has the final say.

The Army game has done more for the exposure of high school football than anything I can think of. And it just seems to be getting better.

HALFTIME

11

HALFTIME

SOME PEOPLE, even close friends, claim I don't have a life, and it's possible that they are right. I am a creature of habit. When I'm at home, my daily schedule reads the same. And when I'm on the road, I follow exactly the same routine every day. But my routines help me enjoy life more than ever before.

A typical day at home always begins at seven in the morning, when I wake up. I don't eat breakfast; I've learned not to need it thanks to my early years on the road. I make calls to coaches. When I'm finished on the phone, I go to my gym in Schaumburg and work out for an hour and a half. I work out five days a week, usually sticking to running and weight lifting. After hitting the gym, I eat lunch at a local restaurant with friends, a group of people I've known for 15 years. I usually eat an Italian beef sandwich and a bowl of soup, and though I usually drink diet soda, I'm making an effort to switch to bottled water.

I spend the afternoon talking to sportswriters and coaches, and I watch film in my home office. While writing about a player for my magazine, I like to watch his film at the same time. I write stories for newspapers, answer my mail, and try to stay on top of the leading prospects, keeping myself updated on their performance or college choices. Nobody can do what I do all by himself. I have a good support staff, a group of mostly unpaid friends around the country who tip me off about promising football players in their areas. My business is all about contacts—over a hundred high school and college coaches and sportswriters, people I trust.

In addition to my more formal sources, I also have a lot of friends around the country who like football. I just ask them to report to me what they read or hear or see about any player in their area. They are very good at it; they send me newspaper clippings and I follow up with research. I ask them to verify information that I have, watch games, and keep their ears to the ground. I don't ask them to evaluate players. I just want them telling me about players in their area who are dong well. Then I'll request film from the player's head coach, arrange for an interview, and make my own evaluation.

Greg Georgelos is my right-hand man. He has worked for me for 20 years. I met him when he was a dispatcher for the Illinois State Police, where he worked with my brother, Terry. He wanted to work for me, wanted to get involved in recruiting. At one time, he organized filming. For 10 years, he filmed games for me. Now he organizes my trips. I give him the names of prospects in areas where I'm traveling and he arranges meetings with players and coaches. He is an ex-Marine who is very good at talking to high school players on the phone. He always seems to be able to get players where I need them, when I need them to be there. When you drive hundreds of miles on one trip and have three or four meetings in one day, timing is all-important. Greg's wife, Michelle, who has taken thousands of my calls over the years, is a saint for putting up with the both of us.

Other Chicagoans whom I rely upon are Ray Caccamo, Jimmy Jack, Tom Romanello, Ed Lewis, and Tom Swider. Jimmy is a former Chicago police officer and author of the book *Three Boys Missing*. He was one of the first on the scene of the Schuessler-Peterson killings in 1955. Romanello and Lewis have been with me for 13 years. They scout the Chicago area by attending high school games. Lewis once covered the

When I was a kid, baseball came before football. As a 5-foot-10, 140-pound 15-year-old, I was named most valuable player of my park league.

Me, my son, Tommy, and Gene Deckerhoff, a play-by-play football announcer and longtime moderator of my weekly recruiting show on the Sunshine Network, photographed in 1995.

Me and my trusty camel in front of the Sphinx and the Great Pyramid in Giza, Egypt, in 1978.

That's me in the middle surrounded by members of my fabulous staff: (left to right) Greg Georgelos, Jim Etchingham, Jimmy Jack, and Tom Romanello.

Me and my longtime friend, Floyd Wisner (right), hooked up with former Oakland Raiders quarterback Kenny Stabler (center) at ESPN analyst Mike Gottfried's charity event in Mobile, Alabama, in 2000.

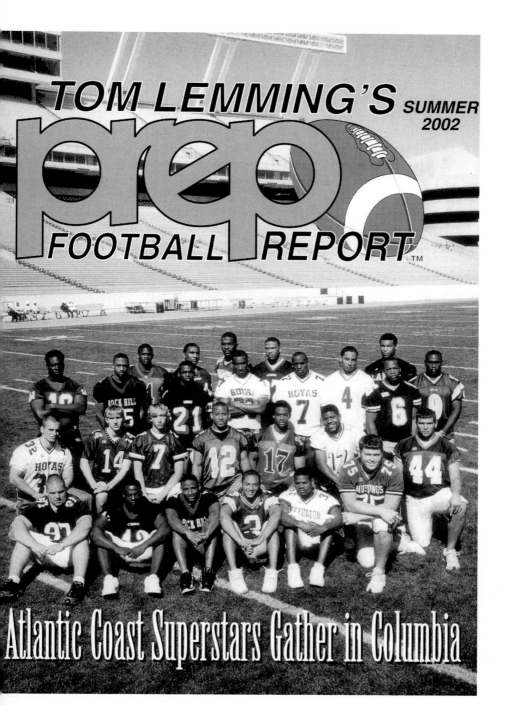

TOM LEMMING'S prep FOOTBALL REPORT™

SUMMER 2002

Atlantic Coast Superstars Gather in Columbia

he front cover of my magazine, circa the summer of 2002. The magazine has come a long vay since 1979. Headliners in this photo include: quarterback Chris Leak (kneeling, middle ow, No. 12), my choice as the national player of the year in 2002; Mario Williams (tallest play-r in the back row, center), the No. 1 selection in the 2006 NFL draft; Blake Mitchell (kneeling, niddle row, No. 7); and Demetris Summers (seated, front row, fifth from left).

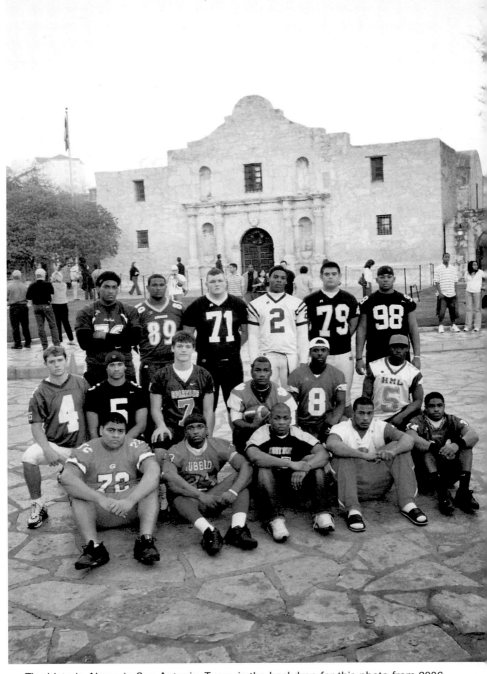

The historic Alamo in San Antonio, Texas, is the backdrop for this photo from 2006. Among the notable players are Jarrett Lee (middle row, No. 4), Caleb King (middle row, center, with ball), Armando Allen (middle row, far right), Robert Hughes (front row, second from left), and Lorenzo Edwards (front row, second from right).

The annual U.S. Army all-star game in San Antonio, Texas, tops off one of my favorite scouting trips each year. Among the standouts who suited up for the 2004 game were Adrian Peterson (standing between Nos. 5 and 11, holding helmet), my choice as national player of the year in 2004, and Zach Miller (kneeling, No. 1).

One of my favorite gathering spots on my annual West Coast trip is Memorial Coliseum in Los Angeles, home of the USC Trojans. Among the many southern California players who posed for this 2004 photo were Mark Sanchez, Marlon Lucky, DeSean Jackson, Ray Maualuga, Averell Spicer, and Kevin Thomas.

I try to photograph many of my magazine covers in front of famous historical monuments to showcase my love of both football and U.S. history. This picture, taken in 2001 in front of Thomas Jefferson's Rotunda at the University of Virginia, featured such notable players as Tyler Palko (standing, No. 3), Jon Lewis (front row, far left), Maurice Stovall (back row, standing behind No. 68), Kai Parham (back row, standing between Nos. 68 and 58), and Ahmad Brooks (back row, standing between Nos. 58 and 21).

orey Stringer was a senior at Warren
arding High School in Warren, Ohio, in
992, before attending Ohio State. He made
y "all-time recruiting team."

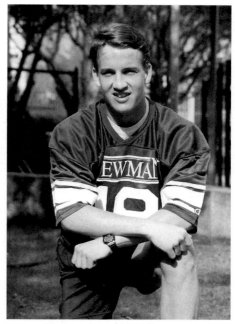

Peyton Manning attended Newman High
School in New Orleans, Louisiana. Manning
and Josh Booty were my choices as co-
national players of the year in 1994.

andy Moss of DuPont High School in
elle, West Virginia, was my choice as play-
r of the year in 1995. From a scouting
andpoint, he was my greatest discovery.

Michael Vick, photographed here in 1998
while a senior at Warwick High School, was
an erratic passer but possessed a strong
throwing arm and blinding speed.

Offensive lineman Jon Ogden made my "all-time recruiting team." He graduated from St. Alban's High School in Washington, D.C., in 1991, and attended UCLA.

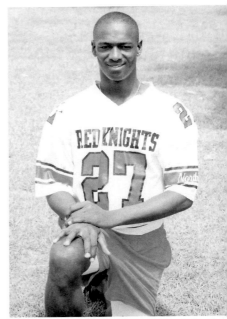

Jevon Kearse was a senior at North Fort Myers High School in Florida in 1994. He went on to become an oustanding line-backer at the University of Florida.

Julius Peppers, photographed as a senior at South Nash High School in Bailey, North Carolina, in 1997, played college ball at the University of North Carolina.

I chose Joe Mauer as my national player of the year in 2001 after his senior season at Cretin-Derham High School in St. Paul, Minnesota. After signing with Florida State he opted to play professional baseball.

Orlando area in Florida for me for seven years before moving to Chicago. Swider, like Greg Georgelos, helps arrange for interviews and gather film. He also is very good at communicating with young people over the phone. Tom and Greg arrange for my one-on-one meetings; I don't talk to players unless they call me.

Steve Raphael, who I've known for 25 years, also helps me. A University of Michigan alum, he lives in Detroit. When it comes to high school football in Michigan and Ohio, Steve is one of the most knowledgeable people I know.

Florida is the most productive recruiting state in the country, and Dave Terhaar, who lives in Clearwater, helps me out by coming up with names from Miami, Ocala, Fort Lauderdale, Fort Myers, Jacksonville, Orlando, St. Augustine, Lakeland, and Tallahassee. I've known him for 27 years. I've also known Jim Kennedy for 27 years. He lives in Philadelphia and covers eastern Pennsylvania and New Jersey, two areas that are consistently fertile when it comes to recruiting.

Dallas Abshire, a former schoolteacher, knows all about Louisiana, which is a tough state for me to navigate because of how difficult it is to get from one town to another. He is Cajun and his name opens a lot of doors. He once coached basketball and knows a lot of high school coaches throughout the state. There always seem to be a lot of good prospects in southern Louisiana, and Dallas finds them for me.

John Cravit, a Californian, is a USC alum and a USC fan. I've known him for 20 years. He keeps me informed on what is going on in southern California—a recruiting gold mine— and always tips me off on anyone who emerges as a prospect on the West Coast. Every year, he arranges my meeting with 30 of the top players in the Los Angeles area at the Coliseum.

Jim Zemula and Matt Egemeier keep me up to date with Nebraska and the Big 12. Jim is a huge Nebraska fan who has his pulse on everything that is going on in Nebraska, Kansas, Oklahoma, and Colorado. I've known Matt for three years. He is a Nebraska student who knows all about Cornhusker football.

In addition to these fine, perceptive people, there are dozens of other individuals I talk to once or twice a year to get information. I don't pay them, but I take them to lunch or dinner during my trips. All of my contacts and friends are honest and they love football, and most of all they enjoy helping kids. I trust their reports. I have a big list of prospects every year and I need to cut it down from 5,000 names to 1,200. They confirm things that need to be checked out. I bounce things off of them. Their feedback and research helps me get that list down to the best 1,200.

I touch base with my friends and contacts, writing and receiving updates, from noon to six in the evening. At that point, I'll either have a frozen TV dinner or go out with my son or with my girlfriend. Then, after dinner, I go back to work until one in the morning. I'll watch college football games on television, or reruns of *Seinfeld*, my favorite show. Otherwise, I don't watch television, and I never watch NFL games. But I will watch a Cubs game whenever I have the chance.

In December and January, I become a movie buff. It's my way of getting away from the hundred or so phone calls I get each day. I haven't taken a real vacation since 1999; I love my job, and I have to keep pace with everything going on in the recruiting world. But I have made a point of trying to spend less time on the phone than I used to.

I average five hours of sleep a night, but that's not nearly as bad as when I'm on the road, when I have to get up at five in the morning and leave at six. Those days vary because each trip is mapped out in advance, but one thing is for sure: I have interviews all afternoon and all night. The last interview always is scheduled for 9:30 at night. I get to a hotel by midnight, hopefully one close to the first scheduled stop in the morning. Before getting some sleep, I try to watch *Baseball Tonight* on ESPN so I can see all the highlights of the day's major league games.

It's an exhausting but exceptionally productive schedule, especially in the last few years since I stopped making a lot of plane flights. In 2000, I had 17 flights on my West Coast trip. I found driving is easier on the nerves and more productive. I am able to go to many more small towns. It also helps my nerves, eases tension, and avoids the weather problems that often cause flight delays. From 1978 to 2001, out of the thousands of scheduled interviews from coast to coast, I never missed an appointment. I've never had a car accident in the 50,000 yearly miles I drive, even though I do a lot of work while driving via my cell phone.

What I have to remember is that there always is somebody I've missed, or a player who has developed since my last trip. That's why there will always be another trip. Even with the help of my staff and nationwide contacts, I can't be satisfied that I have covered everything and everybody because I know I haven't. It's like a painting that is never finished because I am always trying to touch it up. There are always more prospects to find, and there's always a new day to find them.

THIRD QUARTER

12

HITS AND MISSES

IF 50 OF MY TOP 100 RATED PLAYERS go on to become big-time stars in college or play in the NFL, I feel I'm doing a good job. Critics are always eager to remind me of players I've overlooked, or underrated, or overrated, or just plain ignored. That's the nature of recruiting, and I remember that fact when I speak at a college or at any other event. The hit-or-miss aspect of this business is humbling but also motivating—you never know as much as you think you do. Whenever I feel I am on a roll, I think of Barry Sanders and Brett Favre, two guys I overlooked, and I remember that I can always do it better.

In my defense, everybody missed on Barry Sanders. But I should have known better. I was on the road and got a tip about him. I was in Wichita, Kansas—his hometown—but I didn't follow up on the tip. He was small, an injured running back. Someone told me he was a 5-7 tailback and I didn't figure he would make it because he was too small. I wrote about him, but I didn't make him an All-American.

I once mentioned to Francis Peay, then the Northwestern coach, that I had missed on Sanders. He told me not to feel bad. He said he had brought Barry and his brother Byron, a junior college running back, to the campus at the same time. Peay had one scholarship left for a running back and decided to give it to Byron, the bigger of the two. Byron was good but he was no Barry, who ended up at Oklahoma State, the only school to offer him a scholarship.

I missed on Brett Favre, too. I was in Pascagoula, Mississippi, looking at another player. A high school coach told me about a high school quarterback in Kiln, Mississippi, who could throw the ball 100 yards in the air. He said I might want to check him out. I called Favre's father, who was also his coach, and he said Brett was a big-time player and the best quarterback he had seen. I wrote about him but I didn't think he was an All-American; he was an option quarterback and he didn't have great statistics. I didn't stop to see him, which was a mistake. The option offense that his father was running disguised his great ability.

But what is an All-American, and what exactly is it that I'm looking for? My definition of an All-American is someone who has the right size and speed and great production. In high school, he is a difference-maker. He is one of the guys that the other team has to be aware of at all times. When you watch film or attend a game, you know who they are. They leap off the screen at you. You can't take your eyes off them.

When you evaluate some kinds of players, you either hit a home run or you strike out. That's the way it went with Troy Smith of Ohio State. When he came out of Glenville High School in Cleveland, Ohio, he was an unpolished quarterback who looked good at summer camps but didn't have great seasons in high school. He could run and throw and he was very athletic, but he wasn't a prolific passer. He could throw deep, but he didn't possess great accuracy. I wrote about him in my magazine and ranked him as the No. 20 quarterback in the nation. Although Smith wasn't projected to be a super-recruit, he eventually signed with Ohio State, but he wasn't Ohio State's top quarterback choice in his recruiting class. However, Smith developed into a star at Ohio State, winning the Heisman Trophy in 2006. All he needed to do was to become an accurate passer, and now that he's done that, he's in the same class with Notre Dame's Brady Quinn.

One year, I arranged for a lot of kids from Chicago's South Side to meet me at Leo High School on 79th Street. I had seen Chris Zorich, a junior linebacker at Chicago Vocational High School (Dick Butkus' alma mater), play—I'd been so impressed that I rated him as All-Midwest because he was tough and mean on the field. But he played with a chip on his shoulder, as if he had something to prove. I hadn't invited him to the meeting. But Zorich had heard about it and called me to ask if he could come. He's probably the most polite kid I have ever met. Zorich was named to the *Chicago Sun-Times* All-Chicago Public League team. But he didn't make the *Sun-Times'* All-Chicago Area team. I argued for him to be selected for the All-Area team, but the panel of coaches, which picked the 40-man team, didn't vote for him. Now Zorich has been inducted into the College Football Hall of Fame, making him the youngest player ever selected.

Interestingly enough, that same panel of coaches voted for Mike Alstott as the Player of the Year in the Chicago area in 1991. He came out of Joliet Catholic, the same school that sent Tom Thayer to Notre Dame and later to the Chicago Bears. Alstott was a 6-1, 210-pound fullback who led his team to a state championship as a junior and rushed for more than 3,600 yards in his last two years. Like Dick Butkus, he built leg strength by pushing a station wagon down the block. In high school, he had great production, but he wasn't the fastest runner and didn't have the fanciest moves—he was a slashing runner, not a dancer. College recruiters agreed he was tough, but most felt he was too slow. Only Purdue offered him a scholarship. He accepted and went on to become an All-NFL player. I never doubted Alstott's ability. He had a great work ethic. All he did was find a way to the end zone, and in the end, that's what matters.

My biggest discovery was Randy Moss. I saw him as a sophomore in Belle, West Virginia, in the Charleston area. He was known in the Pittsburgh and Charleston area, sort of a local legend. In 1993, when I saw him on film for the first time, it was obvious that he was too good for high school competition, even at that age. Moss was a great athlete, tall and sleek, a 100-meter sprint champion and a basketball star. He had great hands, could jump out of the gym, and looked like he was sleepwalking through games because of his enormous talent. He would hurdle defenders and was having fun doing it. The only glitch was when I'd invited him to our television show at Disney World. His travel ticket had been paid for, but he never showed up. We had people waiting at the airport for him. His mother later told us that he'd decided to go to the mall instead.

That was my first sign that Randy Moss wasn't as mature as he could have been. He signed with Notre Dame but was involved in a fight and had to go to jail, so they dropped him. Then he signed with Florida State and he had to sit out a year. He got caught with drugs in his system so they dropped him, too. He ended up at Marshall for two years, then went on to the NFL. He developed a reputation for being surly with the media, but I always got along with him.

With some players, I didn't even have a chance to hit a home run or strike out because they decided not to pursue football. I deal with a lot of prospects who play both football and basketball. I once interviewed LeBron James; he was an outstanding football player, the No. 1 wide receiver in the Midwest as a senior, one of the best in the country. At the time, I had no idea that he was also a great basketball player. I interviewed him as a junior at St. Vincent-St. Mary's in Akron, Ohio. As a junior, he caught 52 passes for 1,200 yards. He was 6-8 and weighed 240 pounds with a 41-inch vertical leap. I knew he played basketball, but I didn't realize I was looking at one of the future all-time greats.

I'd gone to Akron to see another player at LeBron James' school. I was watching film of both students when LeBron walked into the room. He acted as if he didn't want to be there. I said to him, "I know you're being recruited in basketball, but I think you have NFL potential." He said he thought his options were stronger in basketball because he had just been offered $7 million to play his senior year in Italy on a professional team. I began to realize he was something much bigger than I'd originally thought. Then the coach told me that LeBron was the No. 1 basketball player in the country.

I tried to get his commitment to play in the U.S. Army football game. LeBron agreed. If he played football as a senior, he told me, there was a good chance he'd play in January. I got a handshake that he would consider it. In August, he came to Chicago, broke his wrist in a basketball tournament, and missed the football season. His teammate and the student I'd originally come to see, Sian Cotton, a 6-4, 300-pounder, did play in the U.S. Army game and is now at Ohio State. I still remember driving home from Akron and listening to a sports talk show in Cleveland where they talked about the Cavaliers picking LeBron James in the NBA draft, right out of high school, if they were lucky.

For all those players I've missed, I'm proud to say that I got it right on some pretty remarkable players: Michael Vick, Dan Marino, John Elway, Herschel Walker, Brian Brohm, and Eric Dickerson. I touted Emmitt Smith two seasons before he was the national player of the year. When I first interviewed Vick in Newport News, Virginia, only two schools—Virginia Tech and Syracuse—had expressed interest in the future NFL star. I put him on my All-America team and ranked him among the top 100 players in the nation; he was only 6 feet tall—he didn't have the prototypical 6-5 frame that college recruiters covet in a quarterback—but he did possess a rifle arm. I couldn't overlook a player with his talent, and I'm glad I didn't. All my "hits" were well known in their local areas, before I got there. But I helped to make them national names before anyone outside their areas knew who they were.

As proud as I am of my work, I have to admit I've had my share of embarrassing moments. The worst of them involved

Jim Flynn, the assistant executive secretary of the Illinois High School Association in charge of media relations for many years. We met only once, and I still consider that meeting the most embarrassing incident of my nearly three decades in the recruiting business.

In 2003, a week before the state championship games in Illinois' four largest classes, I decided to go to Champaign to cover the event and write stories for ESPN.com and *USA Today* about what appeared to be a very talented and promising class of juniors. I called the IHSA for a press pass and was told where I could pick it up on the day of the games. I arrived before the first game and asked for my pass. There was an envelope with my name on it—but the pass had been removed.

There must be a mistake, I thought. Someone made a call but got no answer. So I proceeded to then-Illinois coach Ron Turner's office. I was told I could watch the games from his office. Turner had a secretary take me to the press box of Memorial Stadium so I could obtain a pass. The door opened and there was this guy leaning backward, with his feet on a chair in front of him, watching the game. The secretary introduced me to him, telling me his name was Jim Flynn, someone I had never heard of before. I stuck out my hand and said, "Hi, I'm Tom Lemming."

He refused to shake my hand. He said, "I know who you are. You're the one trying to fake credentials that you work for ESPN." I thought it was a joke, so I laughed. He then said, "I'm not stupid. I know you don't work for ESPN. I'm not giving you a pass or allowing you in the press box. So leave."

Even the secretary was shocked. I yelled at Flynn. "What are you talking about?" I said. "Of course I work for ESPN."

"No, you don't work for ESPN," he said. "You're that recruiting analyst and I don't want you here. Leave." He had been the one to pull my press pass. The secretary told me to go back to Turner's office. Flynn called me a liar and kept insisting that I didn't work for ESPN.com. That got me angry; I may be a lot of things, but I'm not a liar.

"You have no right to keep me out of the press box," I told Flynn. "Who the hell do you think you are?"

"Get out of my press box," he said.

I went back to Turner's office. He gave me an Illinois all-access pass. So I went to the field and watched the game. But after that upsetting moment, the day continued to get worse; there was a port-a-potty at the end of the field and my cell phone fell into it.

Later, I was standing at the south end of the field, watching the game, when Flynn came walking towards me.

"What the hell are you doing on my field?" he said. For extra effect, he said it again.

I shouted obscenity at him, to which he replied, "Get off my field." But I refused to move.

"Where did you get that pass?" he said. I told him Illinois had given it to me. "They have no power here," he said. "I run this whole place. This is my field and I want you off. That pass means nothing," he told me. "Illinois has no say on who goes on this field. Get off."

"Make me," I said, acting like a 12-year-old child.

Flynn got on a walkie-talkie and, within a minute, four Champaign police officers surrounded me. One of them said to Flynn, "Should we arrest him?"

"No, just get him off my field," Flynn said. They surrounded me and walked me through the stands with people staring at me. Some spectators yelled, "Don't take him alive" and "Go, Lemming, go." While being escorted off the field, I yelled, "I'll get even with you someday."

After leaving the field, I walked back to Turner's office and watched the game from the warmth of the football office. Then I went home. Later, I wrote stories for ESPN.com and *USA Today*.

I never heard from Jim Flynn again. The entire event was so bizarre and childish. Later, I could have kicked myself for resorting to using a foul word and threatening revenge. But at the time I was furious. I pride myself on not swearing, drinking, or smoking. But that afternoon, he got the best of me. To this day, why he hated me so much is still a mystery to me. I'd never met him before and hadn't even known who he was. I've always felt I deserved an apology from him, but I've never received one.

That may have been the most embarrassing experience of my career, but Illinois' Memorial Stadium isn't the only college football venue that I've been booted out of. Every year, I attend the fall media days and the spring games at several schools. I never call ahead because the coaches know me. That had always been the case for Notre Dame's media day in August. When coach Lou Holtz left Notre Dame in 1995, I wrote a story in *Sporting News* about how I believed Holtz was pushed out of South Bend. And I said the same thing on several radio sports talk shows.

That August, I walked into the stadium with Bob Chmiel, who was the recruiting coordinator at Notre Dame at the time. He said to a guard: "These guys are with me." But the guard stopped me when I told him my name. He clicked on a walkie-talkie and said, "We have Tom Lemming here."

An assistant sports information director then said to me, "You aren't allowed. You didn't call ahead." I told him that I had never called ahead in the past, not at any school when I attended a media day or spring game. "Now you have to, so we aren't letting you in," he said.

I told someone to tell Chmiel that I couldn't get in. Five minutes later, Chmiel came by and told me to meet him by the north gate of the stadium. He brought keys and unlocked the gate and let me in. I tried to be as anonymous as possible, sitting in the stands. But a Notre Dame assistant coach spotted me. He called for an assistant SID, who called security, who then asked me to leave.

I walked across the field, right past coach Bob Davie, who was standing in the middle of the field with the media. We both looked at each other. I'd assumed that he had told them to throw me out. Later in the year, however, he said he had nothing to do with it. When he found out, he said, he got upset with the SID. I didn't visit Notre Dame for 10 years after that experience, except for one occasion when I was invited to sit on Baylor's bench by then head coach Dave Roberts.

Notre Dame fans hated me for writing negative things about their recruiting. I've lost more magazine subscriptions from Notre Dame fans than from any other school. Ironically, I often find myself defending Notre Dame because I have such respect for the school and its football program. A few years ago, a player from Mississippi who was considering Notre Dame was told by a coach from another SEC school, "Don't go there. They'll try to convert you. And they will make you go to church every day." That isn't true. Notre Dame is one of the most liberal schools in the country. A friend of mine attended Notre Dame and had an avowed atheist teaching one of his classes. Notre Dame isn't the conservative, right-wing university that many people believe it to be.

I've had other embarrassing moments, though admittedly not as public or as dramatic as my experiences at Illinois and Notre Dame. Most of them occurred in my early years, when I was an unknown and desperately trying to secure a foothold in a business that was looking for an identity. Some college coaches refused to see me or even take my calls. Joe Paterno and Bobby Bowden, the old-school guys, still won't give me the time of day.

In 1979, one of the first calls I made as I began mapping out my trips around the country was to Clem Gryska, Alabama's recruiting coordinator. He was very cooperative and always recommended players to me. He was the first to tell me about Bo Jackson. I called him three or four times a week. Occasionally, Bear Bryant would pick up the phone because he was the first one in the office every day. I knew it was him right away—there was no mistaking that voice. But I never had a sit-down with him. We only talked on the phone. Whenever

I was in Tuscaloosa, I didn't want to interrupt him; he was the biggest name in college football at the time.

He had a lot of patience with me. "Coach," I would say over the phone, "I want to give Clem this recruiting information," Bryant would answer, "Hang on, let me find a pen." I could tell he was being polite—he wasn't into recruiting at that time of year, and most of the names I gave him were total unknowns. I just appreciated that he wasn't trying to hang up on me. I tried to prolong our conversations. Over a period of a year and half, we talked about six or seven times before he retired after the 1982 season. Of all the people I have talked to in 28 years in this business, he was the only one who gave me that feeling of excitement, just talking on the phone.

As the years went by, I made a lot of contacts with coaches and sportswriters around the country, and I earned their trust. They realized I wasn't a slacker, that I was a hard worker and was dedicated to my job. College coaches eventually realized I knew what I was talking about. I developed a lot of credibility once they knew what I was all about.

But I'm still waiting for an apology from Jim Flynn.

13

CONTROVERSY: THINGS GET PERSONAL

MANY CRITICS SAY that going around the country, talking to players, and watching their films is the wrong way to go about evaluating and ranking prospects. Most analysts use a different method: they get their lists from colleges that do their own scouting, go to a combine, and rank kids according to their personal style. They don't watch films, and if they do, they don't watch films of players from all over the country. I don't need to tell you which method I think is more valid, but the controversy that surrounds all methods is the price of doing business.

Some things hold true no matter how you do your research. If you are in the recruiting business, and you talk with kids, the opinions of schools will come up. Kids want to know about schools, especially academics, graduation rates, chances to play, how many players they have sent to the NFL, and if they stockpile players. The key questions—from both analysts and players—are always the same.

In the world of college football, you can get into trouble, and cause trouble, just by being honest. I am always as honest as I can be with a player when we discuss his future. In all my years, the first thing I always advise players to do is to choose a school that will provide them with good academic opportunities—a school from which they will graduate. But a famous college coach once approached me because he thought I was talking too much about academics. He said that by advising players to go to schools with the highest graduation rates and where they could be sure to get worthwhile degrees, I was pushing kids to certain schools. He said I shouldn't give that kind of advice out because it meant I was prejudiced against schools that didn't graduate players. I laughed, but he was being completely serious.

No matter how you approach your work, controversy will somehow find you. A lot of the criticism directed toward me has involved two Florida State recruits, Lorenzo Booker and Myron Rolle. I've always had a good rapport with Florida State, especially when I did my weekly television show in Tallahassee in the 1990s. I became very familiar with their recruiting and became good friends with Ronnie Cottrell, who was coach Bobby Bowden's recruiting coordinator in the 1990s. He was one of the best recruiters in the country, and he showed me how they went about their recruiting.

Lorenzo Booker was a running back from Westchester, California. He was considered one of the top 10 prospects in the country. I talked to him once, when I met him at a school near the Los Angeles airport with several other players. I called him in December to see if he would play in the U.S. Army game. He said he would.

I didn't talk to him at that game except to say hello. Then ESPN asked me to pick a player who would announce on the February signing day, live on *SportsCenter*. I chose Booker because most of the other top players had already committed. I had originally asked Ben Olson, but he turned me down. Booker, however, loved publicity and he accepted without hesitation. We got into a conversation about which schools he was considering—Washington, Florida State, USC, Notre Dame. I told him that academics should be the most important reason for choosing a school, and he agreed, saying that academics would play a big part in his decision.

In the time between the U.S. Army game and the ESPN signing show in February, I had selected Maurice Clarett over Booker as *USA Today*'s offensive player of the year. I also named Clarett the player of the year in my magazine. The next time Lorenzo and I spoke, I could tell he was upset. He asked me point blank, "So you think that Maurice Clarett is better than me?"

"Yes," I told him. "You are real good, but Maurice is really good, too." Two days before the ESPN show, I called Booker to tell him that he would need to let me know a couple of hours before the show which school he'd chosen so that we could call the correct head coach, Bobby Bowden or Tyrone Willingham (he had narrowed his choice to Florida State or Notre Dame). Booker's uncle called the producer of the show to say Lorenzo was going to Notre Dame. We called Willingham and asked him if he could get to a studio so we could go live on the air after Booker had signed. He said he would.

We were in the studio at ESPN headquarters in Bristol, Connecticut, for the *SportsCenter* show, and 20 minutes before we went live on the air, we got a message from Notre Dame stating that they hadn't received the letter-of-intent fax from Booker, and that Willingham wouldn't go on the air without it. On the set, I told my co-hosts, Chris Fowler and former Pittsburgh coach Mike Gottfried, that something smelled fishy. I said to Fowler, "I think Booker may have lied to us and he's going somewhere else."

Notre Dame continued to send us updates over those next few minutes: there was no letter-of-intent fax to be found. Sure enough, Booker announced he had chosen Florida State. On the air, I couldn't help having a tinge of disgust in my reaction because of the misdirection Booker had given us. Booker apparently didn't like my reaction, and said so much later in a story on Florida State's website.

In the story, Booker denied that he had originally committed to Notre Dame. He said he had never even talked to Willingham or any of the Notre Dame coaches. He said that the reason I wanted to know his college choice in advance was because I'd planned to leak it. And when he'd gone to the ESPN producer, cutting me out of the process, he said I had badmouthed him. He claimed I said he was too small and not that good, and that I'd dropped him in my rankings after he had signed with Florida State. Of course none of that was the case—I never lowered him in my rankings. He was still in my top 10. Lorenzo isn't a bad kid; he's just always loved publicity.

Myron Rolle was a very different case, but it still involved Florida State, which only furthered any existing controversy. Rolle was a defensive back from the Hun prep school in New Jersey. I rated him as the No. 1 junior in the country in February 2005. He had great statistics, and he was 6-2 and weighed 215 pounds and ran 4.5 for the 40. But I hadn't seen 99 percent of the top players in the country at the time. I hadn't begun to make my trips. I made that ranking very early in the evaluation process.

Rolle had gone to the combine in San Antonio. I was told he looked really bad in one-on-one workouts against highly touted Percy Harvin, the best wide receiver in the country, and Jared Norton, a little-known wide receiver from north Texas. Later, after I did my early ratings, I was told that Rolle looked average at best at the combine. I didn't call Rolle again, though he called me periodically to inform me about schools that had made him offers. He'd ask questions and I'd ask questions. He was always very polite and very intelligent. He said his dream was to use football to go to school and become a doctor—a neurologist.

The next time I saw him was at the Elite Combine in New Jersey in May 2005. We invited him to be a guest on CSTV. During our talk, he mentioned the academic schools that had given him offers—Duke, Michigan, Harvard, Stanford, Notre Dame, and Yale. I asked him which way he was leaning. He said he'd narrowed it down to five schools: Florida, Florida

State, Miami (Florida), Oklahoma, and Michigan. He admitted he was leaning toward Florida State.

I was startled. I said to him, "For three months, you've been telling me that you wanted to become a doctor. Why Florida State? What is their track record of producing doctors from the football team as opposed to those other schools?" My honest question led to a story in *ESPN Magazine*. Rolle allegedly told them I was knocking Florida State and pushing Notre Dame. The day the article was published, Rolle called me to apologize for what he'd said in the article. He said his words were taken out of context, that he would never tell people that. I told him not to worry about it. "If it's an honest mistake," I told him, "then I accept your apology."

When my top 100 list came out in August, Rolle was ranked No. 11. He was upset that he was no longer at the very top of my list, although ESPN kept him at No. 1. In early December, he announced on ESPN that he would go to Florida State. Prior to that, though, he'd told the U.S. Army that he would make his announcement at their game. He'd turned his back on the U.S. Army and CSTV and made the announcement on ESPN instead.

I had nothing to do with trying to get him to announce on CSTV or at the Army game; I never talked to him about it, not once. But Rolle believed I was upset with him because he hadn't announced on either of the two mediums with which I was associated. At the end of the year, I ranked him No. 28; I thought I was being generous. He had a good but not spectacular year. He didn't even have a top 10 season in New Jersey. Not one Jersey coach recommended him for All-America honors. He wasn't even named to the all-state team. But Rolle believed I'd lowered his top 100 ranking because I was mad at him, which was just not true. He thought I was trying to get even—something I have never done in three decades of work.

Rolle testified before the Knight Commission, which asked him questions about college football. They didn't ask him anything about me. But an Internet caller asked a question about recruiting analysts and Rolle vented his anger about me, saying that he'd been working to be the best player in the country, but that only ESPN kept him at No. 1. After the incident, I got a call from Tom O'Toole, *USA Today*'s college football writer. He'd been at the Knight Commission meeting, and he wanted my reaction to what had happened.

"This kind of thing happens all the time when kids get upset about rankings," I told him. Then I asked, "Since the question wasn't asked by the Knight Commission, why would you write a story on it?"

O'Toole said, "Because it's news and we don't want to show favoritism toward you." He said everyone would write about it. But actually, only *USA Today* wrote about that particular point the next day. In writing about me, O'Toole passed up a bigger story that Rolle had given to the Knight Commission. Rolle said Florida Governor Jeb Bush had called him and text messaged him about going to Florida State, which is illegal; no supporter of any school can call or text message a player. Other major newspapers picked up on it, including the papers in Atlanta, Orlando, as well as the *Chicago Tribune*, but not *USA Today*.

The NCAA said it was looking into whether Bush had committed a violation. Rolle said he got a text message on his cell phone, but some alumni and friends of Bush said Rolle was lying. Later, Bush admitted to emailing a message to Florida State president T.K. Wetherell, who then showed it to Rolle. If the NCAA did conduct an investigation, we haven't heard the findings, so we're free to believe either side. The dust has settled and Rolle now plays for Florida State. He is a very mature person. I sincerely hope he has the chance to become a neurologist and a Rhodes Scholar, which is what he once told me he wanted to do.

◆　　◆　　◆

Controversy has followed me beyond the confines of Tallahassee. In fact, one of the controversies I hear most about is that I unfairly favor Notre Dame. First off, let me say that I'm not a Notre Dame graduate, and that no members of my family, or any of my friends, have attended the university. I do respect what they stand for in college football, but by no means is Notre Dame the only college program I respect.

In general, Notre Dame is a lightning rod that sparks controversy any time you praise them, especially when you're speaking to anyone from the Deep South. It has been a dominant football program since Knute Rockne and the 1920s, and that kind of long-standing success can breed a lot of contempt. In many ways, Notre Dame is like the New York Yankees: you either love them or you hate them.

There was a time—in fact, most of the time—that Notre Dame didn't like me. I told the truth about Notre Dame's recruiting after coach Lou Holtz left; they weren't recruiting very well, and they didn't go after the great players. Rabid fans actually accused me of being anti-Notre Dame. Many still think so. In fact, three years ago, a representative of NBC asked me if I was anti-Notre Dame because there was only one Notre Dame recruit playing in the U.S. Army game.

People also think I am pro-Michigan and pro-Nebraska and pro-Iowa. Rivals of those schools rip on me because I write recruiting reports for the Wolverine magazine and I say positive things. But I'm not a Michigan guy; if Illinois asked me to write for them, I'd do it, too. I never turn down a school that asks me to write for them. But it only takes the most trivial things to set off fireworks on some campuses. For instance, UCLA fans think I am pro-USC because I take pictures for my magazine at the Los Angeles Coliseum, USC's home field, rather than at the Rose Bowl, UCLA's home field. That's how petty the reasons can get. The plain, boring truth is that I prefer the Coliseum because getting to the Rose Bowl is just too inconvenient.

That brand of pettiness happens everywhere. When I took pictures at Three Rivers Stadium, Penn State fans criticized me because Pittsburgh had played there for one year. When I took pictures in front of Bear Bryant's tower on Alabama's practice field, Auburn fans tore me apart on the Internet. And when I took pictures in front of Thomas Jefferson's famous Rotunda at the University of Virginia after Al Groh became head coach in 2001, it created controversy in the newspapers, and coaches Frank Beamer of Virginia Tech and Phil Fulmer of Tennessee were upset.

One of the reasons why controversy seems to always find me is because I try to ask probing questions, which few people do in recruiting because of their allegiance to certain schools. For example, if a player says education means the most to him and that he wants to go to a school that reflects that, but then he picks a school that isn't known for graduating players, I ask him why. It gets me into trouble, but it's something that should be asked.

Sometimes my involvement in things just gets blown out of proportion. A couple of years ago, one recruiting service rated Jimmy Williams as the No. 1 junior college player in the country. He contacted me during his senior year. He didn't have good grades and I suggested that he enroll at a junior college. He continued to call from time to time. Once, he wanted to get in contact with certain schools, and I gave him the contact information he requested. His high school coach called the schools to set up visits. Later, Williams said I helped him with his recruitment: in a newspaper article, Williams stated that I helped him to go to Virginia Tech. In a sense, that statement is true—I gave him the phone number of Virginia Tech's football office. But despite my very limited involvement, the University of Virginia people were up in arms, saying I was pro-Virginia Tech. That's how things get started.

All I can do is stick to my philosophy: never lie, never charge a penny, and provide anyone who asks with the information they need to contact schools. I didn't lie when it came to Greg Paulus: in 2004, he was the top-rated quarterback in the country. I thought he could be the next Tom Brady, but he was also a highly rated point guard in basketball. After looking at his options, Paulus signed to play basketball at Duke despite his hopes that he could focus on football. A controversy arose when I said he should try to play both football and basketball. I felt he was good enough to be a major star in football, and that he shouldn't have to give up one sport when he wasn't sure which he was better in. I'd stuck to my philosophy, but I'd started some trouble, too.

When you are in charge of something, especially all-star games or selections, and when parents get over-involved, you can get into trouble without even trying. I remember when it came time for me to select the squad for the U.S. Army game. I had to pick between two of the top quarterbacks in the nation: Anthony Morelli from Pittsburgh, and Chad Henne from eastern Pennsylvania. The U.S. Army didn't want two quarterbacks from Pennsylvania, and in the end, I chose Henne over Morelli because I felt he was better; Morelli had a better arm, but Henne had better instincts.

At the end of the season, Morelli's father said I conspired with the coach of the East squad for the U.S. Army game, Bob Palko from western Pennsylvania, to keep his son off the team. It was a big story in Pittsburgh. I had to go on radio shows to defend myself. I hadn't even talked to Palko until December, and even then, I didn't know he was going to be picked as a coach. I was accused of being a Pittsburgh fan. But the simple fact was the U.S. Army only wanted one quarterback from Pennsylvania—they always strive for geographic diversity. The other quarterbacks on the East squad were Brian Brohm of Louisville, who was a Heisman Trophy candidate at the University of Louisville, and Xavier Lee of Daytona Beach, Florida, who started at Florida State.

Sometimes the controversies can get out of hand. In January 2005, it went over the top, and I actually received a death threat. Again, the controversy had its roots in the U.S. Army game. I was at a practice session in San Antonio. ESPN.com conducted a chat room during the week. I arranged for six or seven uncommitted players to take questions from fans during their lunch break. It was promoted as "Tom Lemming's Chat," but I had nothing to do with it after I brought the kids to the press box for the show.

An employee at ESPN headquarters would select questions to ask the players participating in the Internet chat. I had no prior notice of what the questions would be. A question came to Toney Baker, a running back from North Carolina. He was asked, "Would you still consider North Carolina State if they go on probation?" Baker said, "Yes, I would consider them. They are one of my favorite schools."

Later that night, I went to the lobby in my hotel and listened to my messages from home. There were 18 hate-filled voicemails, most of them filled with every swear word known to man. One caller said, "We know when you come to North Carolina in March. This time, you won't make it out of the state alive." Another said, "If Toney Baker goes to Tennessee, we're going to kill you."

Someone advised me to call the police. I called my lawyer, who then called the police in my hometown. They were to call the FBI. After an investigation, they determined that the owner of Packpride.com, North Carolina State's website, had published my private phone number for fans to call. I assume he wanted me to pay the price for committing the supposed sin of asking a question that intimated North Carolina State was being investigated by the NCAA, which it wasn't. The fact is I didn't ask the question, but that didn't stop angry accusations and more controversy.

Fans can get angry when controversies come up, but players get just as upset. Nowadays, there are two things that really seem to stir up their emotions, and where I always get the blame: if they aren't selected to play in the U.S. Army game, or if they feel they haven't been ranked high enough. I get blamed because players don't like to face the fact that they have to earn both these honors on the field.

If there is anything I have learned in my three decades in this business, it's that you have to be thick-skinned. You can't please everyone in college football. If you travel nationally to evaluate thousands of kids and you're honest with them, you will inevitably say good and bad things about schools, and the natural rivals of those schools will viciously attack you. In this business, there are always going to be coaches and players whom I don't like and who don't like me. But I stick to my philosophy, and I never allow my personal feelings to get involved in my evaluations. So far, that's been the best course of action.

14

WAR BETWEEN THE STATES

FLORIDA, TEXAS, AND CALIFORNIA are the leading states in the country for producing high school football talent because of their large populations. They are known as the Big Three. California, the most populated state of all, produces more athletes in football, basketball, and baseball than any other state. The Los Angeles area alone is the largest producer of NFL talent every year. And the success of the USC and UCLA programs has trickled down to the high schools. But if you're a real football fan, you've heard about Texas high school football. It dates back to Sammy Baugh and Doak Walker and Kyle Rote. Still, Florida is even better than Texas at producing talent because every little town has an outstanding football program; in the swamps, football is king. Everywhere you go, the towns seem to close up at five o'clock and everyone heads for the football stadium. In general, there is much more pride and attention paid to high school football in the South than in the North.

Although Florida, Texas, and California, are the Big Three, Mississippi produces more talent per capita than any other state. If not for population, Mississippi would be the leader. Football has prospered there thanks to a warm climate and a lot of blue-collar kids from small and dirt-poor towns in the Delta whose fathers worked in the lumber mills and produced big, tough, scrapping sons. Walter Payton came from Mississippi. So did Jerry Rice, Brett Favre, Marcus Dupree, and Archie Manning.

What I have found fascinating, and difficult, while traveling through Mississippi for the last 28 years is I can't get the top kids together in one location because they are all spread out. Every town is off the main road, I-55, which cuts the state in half from north to south. I have to go through the state three or four or five times each year to find all the good players. This kind of sprawling isn't usually the case. In Georgia, for example, a good number of players can be found in the Atlanta area. In Alabama, several prospects always surface in the Birmingham area. But Jackson, the state capitol, isn't a great producer of talent in Mississippi. Annually, it boasts only two or three of the top 20 prospects in the state.

But make no mistake; Mississippi is a football state. The school system is poorly funded, consistently ranking at or near the bottom in supporting education, but the people take enormous pride in their high school football programs. To people in the South, football is a life-or-death matter. Friday night games attract huge crowds, even in the smallest towns.

In 1981, during one of my first journeys to the South, I met Marcus Dupree. He lived in Philadelphia, Mississippi, the town where three civil rights workers were killed in the early 1960s. I arrived in town and tried to find him. It took forever—this was before cell phones. But Dupree was the biggest name in the country and I had to track him down. He rushed for 5,283 yards and scored 87 touchdowns in his high school career. Although he didn't have good grades, he ended up at Oklahoma and became an All-American as a freshman, then left early to join the new USFL, but his promising career was ruined by injuries. Mississippi was also home to Dwayne Rudd, who I found at South Panola High School in Batesville in the early '90s. He went on to be a standout linebacker at Alabama and played for eight years in the NFL.

Right next to Mississippi is Arkansas, which I believe is the most under-recruited state of all. Unless there is a knockout player, out-of-state colleges rarely spend time there. There are several reasons. Little Rock, the state capitol, is the only big town. And the leading football prospects always seem to have a lot of academic problems. However, there is an exceptionally fast-growing area of the state that ranks with the best areas in the country for producing talented players—the northwest region, around Bentonville (home to Wal-Mart headquarters), Fort Smith, Springdale, and Fayetteville (home to the University of Arkansas).

Over the last three or four years, several blue-chippers have come out of that area, including quarterback Mitch Mustain from Springdale, the national player of the year in 2005. Mustain is the first national player of the year to come from Arkansas. I heard about Mustain at the beginning of his junior year. People sent me information about him. I picked up his name as one of the top 15 juniors in the state from a Little Rock newspaper. He was named to the all-state team as a junior. You could see right away on film that he had great poise and leadership skills, as well as pinpoint accuracy—he hit everyone on the numbers. He was 6-3 and weighed 190 pounds and was mechanically sound and instinctive. As a high school senior, he reminded me of Joe Montana. He was the whole package. In 2006, the list included quarterback Kodi Burns from Fort Smith, offensive lineman Lee Ziemba from Rogers, and tight end Zack Pianalto from Springdale. Football is so big in Springdale that the high school has an indoor practice facility, like many colleges. Strangely, in traveling through Arkansas for the past 28 years, I've learned it is tough to find good players with good grades. But the kids in the northwest region seem to have the benefit of better schools and therefore they tend to have better grades.

Louisiana, like Arkansas, is often overlooked. Players from Louisiana also tend to have poor grades. Also, people don't heavily recruit there because they think all of the good players in the state will opt for LSU. But I have discovered many blue-chippers in the southern part of the state who've gone elsewhere.

Sadly, when I made my annual visit in April 2006, it was like nothing I had ever experienced before. The despair caused by Katrina's devastation was still very evident. Before Katrina, New Orleans was the only town I visited in the United States that doesn't seem like an American city. Instead, when I was in the French Quarter, it reminded me of Amsterdam and Paris—it felt the most European of all American cities. Now I found myself worried that it would never be the same.

For 28 years, I have stayed in New Orleans at a Holiday Inn on Williams Boulevard, off I-10 by the airport. When I arrived in early April, the hotel was closed and windows were broken. The area more closely resembled a ghost town. It was a Sunday and it was clear and sunny. But nobody was on the streets. It was a very weird feeling. I drove into the city to the Louisiana Superdome, avoiding the French Quarter. The families living north of the French Quarter got the worst of it. Brother Martin and St. Augustine high schools suffered the most damage of all.

I continued driving south for a couple of miles to the Jefferson Highway, then to Curtis High School in River Ridge, a suburb. It's a blue-collar area and many businesses were closed. I drove down Airline Highway, which goes through the heart of New Orleans, and went through Metaire, where the New Orleans Saints headquarters are located. I stopped at the Saints' offices and conducted interviews with 25 kids. Saints coach Sean Payton, who was mentioned in my 1981 magazine while playing quarterback at Naperville (Illinois) Central High School, gave me permission to use the building.

I discovered that many top players had been displaced. They had moved on and I would have to meet some of them in Baton Rouge, Monroe, or Lafayette. Chad Jones and David Rue had been students at St. Augustine. Jones had moved to Baton Rouge, Rue to Monroe. They would have been All-

Americans, but Katrina cut their season short. Of course, college recruiters knew about the greatest players and knew where they went after Katrina forced them out of their homes and schools. But many other players couldn't get scholarships because they were borderline prospects and, after being displaced by Katrina, they were simply lost in the shuffle. College coaches didn't try to find them.

One blue-chipper who didn't get lost was running back Joe McKnight of John Curtis High School in River Ridge. He is the best player I've seen in Louisiana in the last 20 years, along with quarterback Ryan Perrilloux, who was my choice as the national player of the year in 2004. McKnight is an exceptional talent; he reminds me of Reggie Bush, with great speed and athleticism.

South Carolina also tends to have players with low grades, but it's also home to some remarkable prospects. In 2005, I got a late tip on Adam Patterson of Columbia, South Carolina, from a scout who was covering North and South Carolina. I saw Patterson's film and liked him. A defensive tackle, he wasn't very good as a junior; I had visited his high school after his junior year and his coach hadn't recommended him as a Division I prospect. But he gained size and improved his quickness, which just goes to show how much a player can develop in his senior year. Patterson went on to play for Michigan.

Another talented player, one who excelled in 2006, was Will Korn of Duncan, South Carolina, one of the nation's top five quarterbacks. When I stopped at the McDonald's in Duncan, I was struck by the sight of pictures of Korn plastered on the walls of the restaurant, like an NFL star. Talk about being a hometown hero—and he was only 18 years old. But that's the way it is in the South; high school and college football mean a lot to them. The schools may not have money for computers or quality teachers, but the people still invest great pride in the athletic programs in their communities.

Of course, other states take their high school football seriously, too. Ohio, Pennsylvania, Georgia, New Jersey, and Illinois are all known for producing great talent. These states are home to a lot of blue-chippers, players that every recruiting analyst is aware of—no matter what state they call home. But much like South Carolina's Adam Patterson, there are some players who, for one reason or another, don't get much exposure as juniors and fail to register on the radar screen. Like Patterson, some of these players are late bloomers, kids who mature emotionally and physically between their junior and senior years, and emerge as genuine prospects.

That was the case for Matt Roth of Willowbrook High School in Villa Park, Illinois. He was only 6-2 and weighed 195 pounds as a junior. But he gained weight and strength before his senior year and emerged as a 6-4, 240-pound defensive end and one of the top 20 players in the nation. He earned a scholarship to Iowa and now is in the NFL.

A more recent example of this kind of prospect is Coby Fleener, from Joliet, Illinois. As a junior, he saw very little playing time, partly because he was playing for one of the most successful high school football programs in Illinois—Joliet Catholic. In fact, he didn't play at all in some games. He possessed height and speed but lacked strength and a hard-nosed attitude. At the end of the 2005 season, when Joliet Catholic coach Dan Sharp was asked to single out the best Division I prospects in his junior class, he never mentioned Fleener. But you couldn't blame the coach for missing this future star: there was no film on him, and he hadn't played enough as a junior to make an impression on anyone.

But Fleener was driven. I had noticed him while watching a game between Joliet Catholic and Carmel of Mundelein on a local cable channel. I saw him make some great catches, and when the announcer said Fleener was 6-6, that definitely caught my attention. I eventually called Fleener and told him he had the potential to get a lot of scholarship offers, maybe as many as 25 or 30.

Fleener decided that he didn't want to sit on the bench as a senior. In the off-season, he added 20 pounds of muscle and reduced his 40-yard time from 4.6 seconds to 4.31. He worked so hard in the off-season that when he showed up for a one-day camp at Illinois State in the summer, he was so impressive that he was offered a scholarship on the spot. In 2006, the 6-6, 220-pounder emerged as one of the leading tight ends in the country. After catching five passes for 100 yards in his team's season opener against another perennial state power, Mount Carmel, at Chicago's Soldier Field, other colleges jumped on the bandwagon. Fleener received more than a dozen scholarship offers from Division I schools, including Nebraska, Arizona State, Minnesota, Colorado, and Kansas, before finally opting for Stanford.

Now Fleener is a poster boy for what determination and dedication can do if you have a burning desire to become a big-time player. As a senior, he caught 40 passes for 700 yards for a 6-4 team. His coach said it was the most dramatic turnabout he had ever seen, from the bench to national recognition, all in one season. Because 99 percent of all recruiting is done during a player's junior year, analysts and college coaches tend to miss any changes that manifest themselves in their senior years. But there are always a lot of Coby Fleeners around the country—players who have gained 20 pounds or have grown three inches when you weren't looking. His case proves that you have to stay on the ball in this business.

15

MEDIA AND THE EVOLUTION OF COMMITMENT

I'VE HEARD PEOPLE SAY that they think there is too much media coverage of high school sports, that 16- and 17-year-olds aren't emotionally or mentally mature enough to handle the headlines or the spotlight. Of course, I may be biased in my opinion, but I don't agree with that. I believe that learning to handle the pressures of the media is tantamount to learning how to handle the pressures of competition.

High school football has always received local media attention. Newspapers published box scores and brief stories on high school events. But sportswriters didn't go into the locker room to get quotes from the players or produce human-interest stories. Slowly, though, things started to change. In Chicago, Taylor Bell, who covered high school sports in Illinois for more than 40 years, began writing feature stories on high school athletes for *The Daily News* and the *Sun-Times*. "Make them walk and talk," Bell's editor, John Justin Smith, told him. For the first time, the paper published special high school pages, personality profiles on athletes, and Game of the Week stories. And they selected All-Chicago area teams in football, boys and girls basketball, baseball and softball. No one else had ever done that before. Then later, in the 1970s, Enos Pennington wrote feature stories on high school athletes for the *Cincinnati Post*. So did Bill Baumgardner in New

Orleans, Bill Buchalter in Orlando, Florida, and Loren Tate in Champaign, Illinois. The national buildup began when *USA Today*, the first national newspaper, began publishing high school sports information in 1982.

Heavy media coverage has its positives and negatives. Some players can't handle it, but a far larger number of high school athletes manage to deal with the notoriety. The national exposure hasn't affected them negatively. We must remember that college football is entertainment, a big business. But I think it's fair to say that 25 percent of players get too much publicity and don't know how to handle fame. It goes to their heads and causes more trouble than it's worth.

I suppose all of this is partly my fault. I was the first to ask kids to conduct exclusive press conferences to make their college commitments. In February 1993, I persuaded Ron Powlus, the national player of the year in 1992, to make his announcement on ESPN. It was a big coup and I helped him into it. That triggered a wave of announcements on live television that has carried over to this day. I admit it's gotten to the point where the coverage is ridiculous. Almost every one of the top 250 football players in the country wants his own TV shot. Players call press conferences that will be covered by four or five TV stations, a handful of radio stations, and five or six newspapers.

Originally, players just announced their decisions to the local press. I recall one great athlete, back in the early 1970s, who was debating between two schools. He couldn't make up his mind. Finally, in July, with both schools still waiting for him to make a decision, his father tossed the two letter-of-intents on his son's bed and said, "Here, sign one of them and let's get it over with. Now." There was no press conference, just a call from his coach to the local media. How times have changed.

Recruiting has become so bizarre. Some players still need to mature and are insensitive toward other people's feelings. They don't realize that if they can't live up to the hype, it could be embarrassing. One player in Texas called a press conference and signed his letter-of-intent in a hot tub. In 2005, Antonio Logan-El, a player who had already been committed to Maryland for over a year, received a lot of media attention when it was speculated that because of Penn State's outstanding season, he was considering them. A week before his official announcement, he called Maryland to invite them to his signing event and he requested tickets for a Maryland basketball game, which they gladly gave him. Imagine everyone's surprise when, in front of everyone, Logan-El announced for Penn State.

But it is hard to recall any announcement that had more glitz and glitter attached to it than when quarterback Jimmy Clausen, the nation's top-rated player who committed to Notre Dame, arrived at the College Football Hall of Fame in South Bend, Indiana, near the Notre Dame campus, in a white stretch Hummer limousine with a police escort and public relations firm in tow. It had all the trappings of a Hollywood premiere.

I should start by saying that Jimmy Clausen is one of the five best high school quarterbacks I have ever seen. He has all the tools—ice water in his veins, a big-time passing arm, poise, leadership skills—but the key thing that separates him from all others is his instinctive and uncanny knack for putting the ball exactly where it belongs regardless of a pass rush or the play call. I first became aware of him when a friend of Clausen's family mailed me a tape during Jimmy's sophomore year. I was shocked that he was only a sophomore—he already played better than most seniors. In one film, he was throwing with NFL players at a combine. With their helmets on, I couldn't tell the difference between Clausen and the NFL quarterbacks. That's how good he is.

So at the start of his junior year, I rated him as the No. 1 junior in the country. And he didn't let me down. At the end of the season, he was still No. 1. In fact, he had further separated himself from everyone else; he passed for more than 4,000 yards as a sophomore and 3,665 yards and 57 touchdowns as a junior. As a senior, he completed nearly 70 percent (194 of 281) of his passes for 3,428 yards and 49 touchdowns with only six interceptions. To me, he was the clear-cut choice for best player in the nation. But one recruiting service selected running back Marc Tyler, Clausen's teammate who'd committed to USC, as its top player. And another recruiting service picked defensive lineman Marvin Austin. One service rated Clausen as the fourth best player. When you build up someone so high, people sometimes feel he has to be brought down. So they look for flaws—but Clausen has very few of them.

His commitment announcement, however, was a bit off the wall. The day before the press conference, a Los Angeles public relations specialist had sent an e-mail to inform the media that a "major college football recruiting announcement" would be made the next day at the Hall of Fame. *The Los Angeles Times* reported that an NFL agent had organized the press conference but the report was later denied. Clausen's father also denied that he had anything to do with orchestrating the event.

The announcement was timed so that it would come a few hours before Notre Dame's annual Blue/Gold game. More than five hours before the game, almost all of the seats in a second-floor room were filled with media members, sportswriters, family, friends, Notre Dame boosters, and Notre Dame football fans. Behind the front row were eight television cameras. ESPN covered the event live. It wasn't a press conference; it was a pep rally—Hollywood style.

I saw Clausen 20 minutes before he had to go to the Hall of Fame for the announcement. He was wearing his high school jersey, not a suit and tie, for a picture with a dozen other blue-chippers at a field off the campus, three miles south of the Hall of Fame. I'd taken a picture with him earlier in the day, which ended up appearing in my magazine. Clausen is a really good kid, but in the days following his announcement, the media turned on him, like I knew they would, because they felt he'd gotten too much publicity. Some observers, including *The Los Angeles Times*, skewered him for what was perceived by many as the most bizarre, most over-hyped recruiting announcement ever made. I think part of it came from the built-in dislike some people have for Notre Dame. It was like Alex Rodriguez choosing to play for the New York Yankees; he knew everyone would be against him, that his decision would be panned in the media.

Eric Sondheimer of *The Los Angeles Times* wrote: "Sportswriters and fans have been given the green light, and they're going to treat [Clausen] as they would any high-profile college or pro athlete. That means every mistake is open to ridicule and every decision made on or off the field is fair game for scrutiny." Greg Couch of the Chicago Sun-Times wrote: "We officially have gone insane, dressing up our kids to play pretend rock star, then taking the whole thing seriously, with grown-ups giving standing ovations. Someone needs a spanking here, and I think it's the adults." Dennis Dodd of cbssportsline.com reported: "What happened in South Bend on Saturday thrust the utter absurdity of the recruiting process to another dimension."

Afterward, I said Clausen's commitment event sent a message that Notre Dame was back, that coach Charlie Weis' presence means the Irish will once again be seriously contending for the best players in the country, as they did when Lou Holtz was in South Bend. Couch took me to task on that one. "No, no, that's not the message," he wrote. "I'd say the message is we've gone way overboard in the way we're recruiting kids to play college sports."

Part of me did think that the press conference might have been overkill. I asked Marvin Austin and several other All-America players, "Don't you think it's a bit too much?"

"Are you kidding?" Austin said. "I'd give my right arm to have my announcement on ESPN." The players loved it. So I began to see the event in a different light, why it was so attractive to the kids. It was a stroke of genius for whoever thought of it—Weis, Clausen, his father. In the wake of Clausen's announcement, Notre Dame got four or five commitments in the next two weeks. All of them said they loved the attention and atmosphere that Clausen brought to Notre Dame with the ESPN cameras. In the eyes of the recruits, it was pure magic. You can't penalize kids who love the exposure in newspapers, radio, television, and the Internet, and do a good job with it.

I'm always surprised when a high school coach won't permit his players to talk to the media after games. Kids should be exposed to the media at the high school level so it isn't culture shock when they get to college. Some coaches are control freaks and don't have faith in their kids, so they don't allow them to talk to the media. It doesn't benefit the player. Being in the spotlight early prepares them to say the right things, the politically correct things. Some colleges even hire public speaking professionals to teach their athletes how to deal with the media. College freshmen should already be well spoken when it comes to handling a press conference, and they can learn those skills in the crash course that is the recruiting process.

When Kareem Abdul-Jabbar was still Lew Alcindor and playing at UCLA, he wasn't permitted to talk to the media by legendary coach John Wooden. At the time, he didn't think anything of it. He was only interested in playing and winning. Later, however, when he moved to the NBA, he realized that his lack of communication skills were a hindrance to his development. It was, he said, the only regret of his college experience.

Of course, the media should recognize when a player is modest, shy, or not prepared to meet the media. Nobody wants to embarrass a player by exposing his shortcomings on national television. Orlando Pace was shy, afraid to fly in airplanes, and had trouble relating to the press. Ricky Williams wore his helmet while talking to the media. And Chris Zorich talked with a pronounced stutter coming out of high school. After four years at Notre Dame, he never stuttered again. Now he is a media darling.

Peyton Manning and Emmitt Smith were masters of public interaction. Of course, Peyton grew up in an atmosphere where his father had been exposed to enormous media pressure as an All-America quarterback at Mississippi and later as the face of the New Orleans Saints franchise in the NFL. Some, however, are awestruck by the media blitz and don't handle it well at all. Maurice Clarett, the national player of the year in 2001, had trouble dealing with people on the phone. It wasn't surprising that he got into trouble after his Heisman-like freshman year at Ohio State. Clarett needed someone to give him good advice. He needed more discipline to handle his early success. Instead, he listened to people who steered him in the wrong direction. And he hasn't recovered. It's a sad situation, one that I hope other prospects will learn from.

One of the biggest negatives associated with the heavy media coverage is the surge in de-commitments. There were more than 100 de-commitments—players kids who made verbal commitments to a college, then changed their minds and went elsewhere—in college football last year alone. The trend started 10 years ago, to a much smaller degree, but it keeps snowballing. It gets worse every year.

There are a lot of reasons for de-committing. Some switches are understandable, such as when a coach is fired or a recruit discovers he has been lied to about other players coming in. But part of it is the product of a recruiting process run amok. It's also a matter of lost and shifting values, not just in sports but also in society as a whole.

In the old days, a handshake sealed a promise you could not break. Your word was your bond. But these days, a player's word means very little. Most players feel they can renege on a promise because they don't have pride in their word. As long as they've found an excuse, they see nothing wrong with going back on a verbal agreement. Today, the word commitment, as it pertains to college recruiting, has come to mean the school that has landed a verbal commitment has the lead in the wooing of an athlete. There is no such thing as a 100 percent early commitment anymore.

It's not entirely the player's fault, though. You can't blame them for loving the attention. They are often overwhelmed by scholarship offers, invitations to visit college campuses, and phone calls from big-name coaches. Too many players get poor advice from parents and high school coaches. They're encouraged to jump at the first offer, which is possibly the worst thing they can do, unless they're absolutely sure that it will be best situation for them, or that it's the only offer they'll get. And factor this in: players who weren't ready to commit early and opted to wait were rewarded by receiving more offers. The ones who committed early had only one or two offers. I believe they shortchanged themselves.

Interestingly enough, de-commitment is a one-way street. Colleges hardly ever drop players once they commit. But colleges trigger de-commitments by recruiting more and more players sooner than later. Colleges prefer it when players commit early. But after a prospect commits, they continue to recruit other players, hoping they might sign an even better player at his position. Meanwhile, other colleges continue to recruit the original player, trying to persuade him to change his mind by pointing out they can offer something better. The process goes around and around. When a player changes his mind and chooses another school, but that school already has a commitment from someone else who plays the same position, completely different schools will call the originally committed player to point out the conflict. Then that player begins to waffle, leading him to make more visits and choose another college. It has gotten out of control.

I have been accused of encouraging kids not to commit early. I do, but only if asked directly. Commit early if that is your choice, I tell them, but do it only if you are prepared to stick to your decision. Keep to your word. I see very little that's positive in making an early commitment. It's like marrying the first girl you meet. It takes time to make such an important decision. The winds of recruiting blow hard; you could commit in March of your junior year and the college coach could be gone by February of your senior year. If you're academically inclined, why not check out as many schools as possible? Most players haven't given a lot of thought as to what their major will be, what they will do after they are no longer playing football. The extra time helps them figure things out, and they can make a more informed choice once they know what they want to study. It is also very important to visit the college campus to see how you will fit in socially, and that can't happen when you make an unofficial visit in the spring or summer, when students aren't there. To make the best choice, a player should wait until they are 100 percent sure. To be able to keep their word, they should make educated decisions, which takes time and legwork.

Almost all bad decisions are made early on because players aren't practical and don't listen to the right people. Instead, they listen to people with ulterior motives and personal agendas. Ron Powlus is the classic example of someone who made a bad football decision. Powlus, a quarterback from Berwick, Pennsylvania, was the national player of the year in 1993. Beano Cook, ESPN's college football sage, predicted that Powlus would win two Heisman trophies at Notre Dame. He had Dan Marino-type potential, with a strong arm and quick release, but he needed to go to a school that would groom him in a pro-style offense. Powlus was a straight dropback passer, but he opted to play for Lou Holtz, who was running some option offense. His style wasn't suited for the option, but the lure of Notre Dame and Holtz' aura attracted him to South Bend. It never worked out for him. He picked Notre Dame over Pittsburgh, which probably would have been a better choice for him athletically.

Dan Kendra of Allentown, Pennsylvania, a quarterback who was the national player of the year in 1995, also made a bad choice. In what I still believe was the best class ever, Kendra was picked over Randy Moss by some. He could have gone to any passing school in the country but, after initially committing to Penn State, he changed his mind and opted for Florida State. One reason that led him to change his mind was that Bobby Bowden, while head coach at West Virginia, had coached Kendra's father. But Florida State already had Thad Busby and Danny Kanell playing ahead of him. They quarterbacked for four years, and Kendra was eventually switched to fullback as a fifth-year senior. He never developed into the quarterback that recruiters had projected.

Quarterbacks usually make the worst decisions because they have to go to a program that works around their talent, not where they can fit in, which is what happened to Hall of Fame member Troy Aikman. A native Oklahoman, he was swept off his feet by Sooner coach Barry Switzer, and so signed with Oklahoma. Switzer told him that he would switch to a pro-style passing game to accommodate Aikman's passing skills. But Switzer went back to the wishbone, and Aikman, feeling like a fish out of water and realizing that his chances to excel at an option offense were slim to none, transferred to UCLA.

After committing to Arkansas, Mitch Mustain got cold feet because he thought the Razorback offense wasn't suited for his preferred style of play. So he de-committed and said he wanted to go to Notre Dame. But coach Charlie Weis had promised that he would sign only two quarterbacks, and he already had commitments from Demetrius Jones of Chicago's Morgan Park, and Zach Frazer of Mechanicsburg, Pennsylvania. So Arkansas coach Houston Nutt hired Mustain's high school coach, which lured Mustain back into the fold. Later, though, he transferred to USC.

Last year, Jevan Snead of Stephenville, Texas, committed to Florida. He was rated among the top five quarterbacks in the nation. He switched to Texas after Florida kept pursuing Tim Tebow, whom coach Urban Meyer eventually signed. Meyer had rated Tebow ahead of Snead in his evaluations. So Snead opted for Texas. He played five games as a true freshman, and then transferred to Mississippi. Similarly, Ryan Perrilloux, the national player of the year in 2004, originally committed to Texas, where he would have sat behind Vince Young as a freshman, then started the following year. But after appearing in the U.S. Army all-star game, Perrilloux switched to LSU. It appears to have been a case of bad judgment, because he languished on the bench for two years behind JaMarcus Russell.

Some de-commitments turn out for the best, however. Last year, Emmanuel Moody, one of the top-rated running backs in the country, committed to Texas, then switched to USC, where he made a strong contribution to coach Pete Carroll's program as a freshman. He switched because he felt he would play sooner at USC once Reggie Bush and Lendale White left. He was right.

Hopefully, the mass of players following in his de-commitment footsteps will be half as lucky.

16

STEROIDS

MOST HIGH SCHOOL ADMINISTRATORS don't feel that steroids are a big problem in their programs—at least, not as big a problem as they are in college—so they don't think it is necessary to test students for them. For the most part, I think they're right; steroids aren't a *big* problem in high schools. But they are a problem. Steroid use is more prevalent in high schools than most people care to admit. Today, it isn't as much of an epidemic as it was in the 1980s. However, because of new masking agents, it is now easier to obtain and use steroids without being detected.

I'd estimate that at most, 10 to 20 percent of all high school football players take or have taken steroids. Players can order the drugs online through the black market. Sometimes they can get them at private gyms. More would take steroids if they could afford them, and the public would then probably pay more attention to this issue. But for the most part, it takes a well-connected, well-to-do player to get steroids.

The athletes who take steroids do so because they know they won't get caught; high schools argue they can't test for the drugs because the process is too costly. Even in college programs, players are sometimes told far in advance when testing will be conducted. When it comes to investigating current players, coaches and NFL officials try to keep their heads in the sand, even though football is a logical sport for steroid use because the drugs build up muscle mass. But the public is currently paying attention to steroid use in major league baseball—so far, football has received a free pass. Over the last 20 years, high schools and colleges have distributed a lot of educational material on the subject, but steroids haven't gone away.

Players also believe steroids will make them better athletes on the field. The drugs make it easier for them to gain that extra 20 pounds of muscle that might push them into scholarship contention. Two main things players taking steroids hope to improve on most of all are 40-yard dash times and explosiveness. Explosiveness is how fast and with how much force a player comes out of his stance, while 40-yard dash times show how a player maintains that speed for a longer distance. Enhancement in those two aspects could mean the difference between a scholarship to a Division I or a Division II school. Steroids provide a psychological boost, too, because they give an athlete a feeling of invincibility.

When I began scouting and evaluating football players, there were no steroids. There were also no personal trainers, no speed gurus, and no fitness centers. Players invented their own strength training routines, such as when Dick Butkus pushed a car around the South Side of Chicago to condition his legs. Compared to what players are doing today, those were the Dark Ages. Weight training is now a year-round activity. In the South, some weight rooms are as large as some colleges. They employ strength coaches to oversee the facility and plan workouts for the athletes. It is as professional as you can imagine.

The phenomenon of personal trainers seemed to start around the mid- to late 1990s. They can be expensive. Some families invest around $2,000 on personal trainers and speed trainers for their sons. But before committing to such a big— albeit profitable—investment, the key is to know whether or not that player even has the potential to be a Division I athlete.

Some parents are completely unaware of their sons' limits; some just don't want to admit those limits exist. But if a player does have that kind of potential, and his parents can afford it, they should employ a personal trainer or speed trainer to help their son enhance his performance. At the very least, the added professional help will get their son in terrific physical condition before the season. And at best, it can improve his strength, speed, and explosiveness, things that college recruiters are looking for. If a family has the money, it's a win-win situation.

In the 1960s, professional football players weren't paid millions of dollars, so they needed to work off-season jobs to feed their families. They sometimes got out of shape during that time, and so used preseason training in the spring or fall to get back in peak physical condition in preparation for the new season. But times have changed.

Professional athletes make a lot more money now, so their off-season job is to stay in top physical condition. And that practice has trickled down to colleges and high schools. If you allow a player to just be a kid during the summer, so the argument goes, he will fall behind his competitors.

Some players, after they have reached their peak in training, still may not feel they are good enough. They may feel that steroids are just the next logical step. But players need to be realistic. They need to understand what they are honestly capable of doing. If he isn't tall enough or doesn't have a big enough frame to carry 300 pounds, he must realize the extra weight isn't good for him—that he's just not made to be that big. But it's a hard fact to face, especially when a scholarship is on the line, and a growing number of high school players are willing to take the long-term risks associated with steroid use in order to meet college standards for a scholarship.

When I'm looking for information on steroids, conditioning, personal training, sports performance enhancement, and other things that can positively or negatively impact an athlete's body, I seek the expertise of John McNulty, the CEO and co-owner of Cynergy Fitness and Sports in Lake Forest, Illinois. During the course of one year, he works with 200 to 300 individuals from age 7 to 80. He has trained professional, college, and high school athletes. Everyone endorses his program. I've never heard a negative thing said about him or what he does.

McNulty agrees with my assessment that steroids are more widely used at the high school level than many people care to admit. He's seen surveys that reveal a 67-percent jump since 1995-96. When faced with a player who thinks steroids are the way to easy success, he reminds them that gaining short-term strength leads to long-term bodily damage. A 16-year-old heart isn't ready to suddenly handle a 300-pound body, and steroids lead to liver damage, joint problems, and cramping or pulled muscles.

McNulty says he has never encountered a high school student in his training facility who has shown signs of steroid use. But he still always looks for those signs—irritability, mood swings, nervousness, acne, a very drastic increase in muscle and weight, breast enlargement in boys, facial hair growth and deepening voice in girls. Because there are so many supplements on the market today that are legal, McNulty looks at past history to determine if an athlete might be taking steroids. He examines how they have progressed up to that point. For example, a weight gain of 20 to 30 pounds isn't that outrageous in a year based on today's training techniques. But McNulty also looks at a player's strength gains. A 180-pound teenager who bench-presses 200 pounds, but then gains 30 pounds in a year while his bench-press goes up to 320 or 330 pounds, would send up a red flag.

McNulty advocates teaching players early on—before they even reach high school—about proper nutrition and how to properly develop the body. In high school, he says, the body must be prepared to perform genetically without steroids—

but it doesn't mean the individual will be a college or professional athlete. And that's just reality.

Another trainer dedicated to helping players reach their potential while staying drug free is David Buchanan, president of ProSport Training and Rehabilitation, based in Rolling Meadows, Illinois. Dave Buchanan recalls a kid who walked into his facility and admitted he was on steroids; as a high school freshman, he weighed 160 pounds. As a senior, he weighed 240. Buchanan points out that recruiting manuals list the preferred weights for Division I players by position. Players sometimes turn to steroids because they feel they must match those weights to play. And the quickest way to gain muscle weight is to use steroids.

Steroids have made champions out of second-stringers, Buchanan says, but the body structure isn't made to take that abuse. He and McNulty see more players breaking down, more injuries, more ACL tears. Buchanan says no major study has been done on the effects of steroids that take the bigger dosages most athletes use today into consideration. "We don't know how bad it can be," he says. But when you see professional athletes breaking down, it gives a sense of the kind of damage going on.

There is no easy approach to gaining weight and getting faster. It doesn't come from an over-the-counter pill or an injection. It takes hard work to match the performance of the best college athletes—there just isn't a quick way to get there that doesn't have harmful repercussions. Buchanan advises that players look at a multipronged approach that includes proper diet, sleep and rest, training, speed, and weight. It is important to find the right people, especially if your goal is to obtain a college scholarship. A player can hang his hat on the wrong guy or the wrong program and ruin himself. But one thing is always certain: no athletic plan should involve steroids.

17

THE STORY OF TWO MICHAELS

IT ALL BEGAN WITH A TELEPHONE CALL from Michael Lewis, a writer for the *New York Times*. When he called, he said he was doing research for a book on a promising football player named Michael Oher from Memphis, Tennessee. Lewis said that while talking to people who have had an impact on Oher's life, my name kept popping up early and often in the conversation.

Lewis wanted to know more about me. He kept calling me—about 20 phone calls in all—to get more background material on me and how I discovered Oher, how I approached him and what I had found out. He had already talked to several people, including Oher's coach, about me. Finally, we arranged to meet at a restaurant in Memphis, a Taco Bell owned by his boyhood friend Sean Tuohy, located across the street from the University of Memphis campus. It was Tuohy who had tipped off Lewis about Oher.

We talked for about 90 minutes. I couldn't talk longer because I was in the middle of my southern trip and had scheduled an interview session with a group of players from the Memphis area. At the time, I thought I was doing Michael Lewis a big favor by agreeing to an interview during a busy time of the year for me. To be honest, I didn't know who Michael Lewis was, and of course, I didn't know this was going to be a big book. But as it turned out, he did me a big favor by putting me in his book. It would end up bringing a lot of attention to my work.

Lewis wanted to know the facts about my background. He also wanted to verify what I had said earlier and what others had said about me. He was very concerned with accuracy, which I appreciated. He was smart, personable, and very thorough, very much at ease with a stranger, very laid back. I felt very comfortable with him. In fact, I was more at ease with him than I am with most writers I meet because many of them don't have a sense of humor. They are all business and keep rehashing things. Lewis seemed to enjoy what he was doing and made me feel as though I were talking to someone I had known for years, not minutes.

Like me, Lewis had stumbled upon Oher virtually by accident. In the fall of 2003, while passing through Memphis, he called Tuohy about a magazine article he was writing about his former high school baseball coach. In passing, Tuohy informed him about Michael Oher. At the time, Lewis didn't pay any attention. A few months later, however, his friend told him that Oher was being hounded by college football coaches and he was being projected as a future NFL left tackle, a highly prized position that protects the quarterback's back side. Finally, coaxed by his friend and his wife, Lewis decided to pursue the story.

Lewis, who also wrote the best-selling book *Moneyball*, interviewed me in March 2005, a year after I had gone to Memphis to interview Oher, then a student at Briarcrest Christian High School, a small private school with no history of producing Division I football players. I'd been sent a film of Oher, but I didn't know anything about him. I'd filed it in with hundreds of others prospects I'd consider in my Louisiana-Mississippi trip.

I looked at the film a few months before heading south. In the package, Oher was described as six feet, five inches tall and 350 pounds. That immediately caught my attention. You don't find many players that big, even in the NFL. When I looked at Oher's film, I didn't see a great player. But I saw an athlete. He wasn't dominating or polished, but he was big and moved well. Anyone who is that big and moves that well has All-America potential. I wanted to know more about him. Because of his size and promise, I put his name at the top of my top 200 list and mailed my list to several colleges.

But literally finding Michael Oher was another matter. When I contacted high school coaches in the Memphis area about Oher, they either didn't know who he was or didn't think he was any good. When I entered his name into Internet search engines, they yielded nothing. He had received absolutely no recognition in the local newspaper. The only proof I had that Michael Oher even existed was a grainy videotape. Even so, I had already picked him to be on my All-America team—and I hadn't even met him yet.

Oher didn't even have a phone number. Nobody seemed to know where he lived. Officials at his high school, suspicious at first of a stranger from Chicago asking questions about the player, finally arranged for me to meet him at the University of Memphis' football facility. It was unlike any interview I have ever done. There were 10 other recruits in the room. I was there for a couple of hours, but I spent most of my time with Oher because he was so uncooperative. I was determined to communicate with Oher and obtain the information I was seeking.

I had two sheets of paper, two questionnaires, the U.S. Army's and mine. I asked for the usual information—size, statistics, grades, describe your best game, describe yourself. And I asked the usual questions: What colleges are you interested in? What do you want to major in? Where do you think you'll be in 10 years?

Total silence. He didn't say a word. He just shrugged his shoulders. I've interviewed thousands of kids over the years, but this was the first and only time that a kid had refused to talk to me, or to even fill out the questionnaires. He didn't write anything on either sheet except his name.

I thought he was acting indifferent toward me. He wouldn't look at me in the eye. I talked to him for over an hour and couldn't get any reaction. He answered every question with a curt "yeah" or a "no." I thought he was aloof, cocky. But I didn't think he was unusual. I frequently interview kids with too strong a sense of self-entitlement. They feel they should be getting publicity. They are ungrateful. And after that interview, I felt Michael Oher was one of them. I marked him off the list for the U.S. Army All-America Bowl; when I'd talked about it with him, he'd acted as if he didn't want to play. Still, I listed him as the top left tackle in the country, even though I was disappointed in his interview.

In March 2004, I began to tell schools about him, before the college recruiters were allowed to visit prospects. I put his name in my magazine and listed him as a first-team All-American. But I heard nothing from him or his school until later that year. In November, his high school coach called and asked why Oher hadn't been invited to participate in the U.S. Army game. I told him that Oher hadn't even bothered to fill out the questionnaire, that I thought he was indifferent about the whole thing.

Then came the information that explained everything. The coach said that Oher had been scared to death during our meeting. Oher had been afraid that I would find out he had trouble writing, that he had trouble communicating with adults. What I had perceived as arrogance, he said, was actually a scared little boy in a big man's body.

What never crossed my mind at the time was that Michael Oher had no clue who I was or why I was there. He never even thought of himself as a football player. The recruiting process was as foreign to him as the Russian language. After his coach explained Oher's background to me, I began to understand his behavior. He'd recently moved, and he'd slept only on floors up until beginning high school. I felt terrible about not realizing sooner in the process that Oher couldn't read or write, that I hadn't taken the time to find out more about his personal background.

I knew we had one opening left in the U.S. Army game, at center. Oher had never played the position before, but I got permission from Garrett Shea, who supervises the game, to add Oher to the roster as a center—if his coach could teach him to play center in one month. His coach worked with him on snapping. So Oher played center in the game. He had an opportunity to mingle with the best players in the country. He stayed at the Westin Hotel and was treated like royalty. The opportunity showcased his talent, and he ended up attending the University of Mississippi, where he was a freshman All-American. He was a sophomore last season and, from all accounts, continued to make a name for himself. He has the potential to be a first-round draft choice in the NFL, but that will come down to his work ethic—how hard he wants to work to achieve that goal.

I haven't seen Michael Oher since the U.S. Army game. So imagine my surprise when a producer representing Bryant Gumbel's HBO Sports show called me, wanting to do a story based on the experience. The producer had read an excerpt from Michael Lewis' soon-to-be-published book in *New York Times Magazine*. The story was about Michael Oher, but it had mentioned me, and the producer of Gumbel's show wanted to learn about my background and how I had helped other players in the past. I was flattered by the article. I had been quoted accurately. I got over a hundred calls from across the country. And I was even more flattered by *The Blind Side*, which devotes an entire chapter to me.

In September, a friend of mine picked up a copy of the book the day after it arrived in bookstores. He had read a few chapters and noticed I was in it. So he called me to let me know about it. The first time I opened the book, I read a passage that said, "Michael Oher didn't realize who this strange little man was." I immediately became insulted by the use of the word little; I weigh 200 pounds. I said to myself, "What is he talking about?" But size is relative. From Michael Oher's perspective, everyone else certainly looks little.

Later, I had time to read the entire book. I was blown away. It's nice to be mentioned in a book, especially in such a positive way. I had been doing this work for years but apparently no one was aware of it. Suddenly many people—coaches, fans, sportswriters, networks—called to tell me they had read the book and wanted to chronicle what I'd been doing. They acted as if they had just discovered me after 30 years.

I didn't know how far-reaching the book would be until I saw Michael Lewis on *The Colbert Report* on Comedy Central. I realized then that everybody was reading the book. Lewis was a best-selling author, and this book was going to be on the *New York Times* best-seller list. It's amazing how a book can get your name out there like that. I've been in *USA Today* about a thousand times and I thought people knew me, but I guess they didn't. Meeting Michael Lewis turned out to be a big break for me. His book has given me a lot of national publicity. It validated what I've been doing for the past 28 years. A lot of people knew I was making trips but didn't know what I was really doing—that I was helping a lot of kids.

I've been told that Hollywood has bought the movie rights to the book, and that it could be made into a motion picture. I wonder who will play me: Brad Pitt, Tom Hanks, or Mel Gibson? When I got to Memphis last October, I ran into the Tuohy family and Oher's teacher. They said they were surprised that I looked so young. They said they were expecting a much older man. We'll see what Hollywood decides when it comes to my age.

The truth is, until I met Michael Lewis at that Taco Bell restaurant in Memphis, I had no idea about most of the Michael Oher story. I only knew about the football side. I thought Michael Oher was another spoiled, indifferent athlete who had been given too much too soon. In reality, he was a shy street kid who had no family. He'd just moved into a white family's home and was adjusting. Everything that was happening to him was a shock, including meeting me. But Michael Lewis helped to open my eyes. It's a story I'll never forget. And I'm proud to be part of it.

FOURTH QUARTER

18

SIGNIFICANT MOMENTS, SIGNIFICANT PEOPLE

IN 1963, when I was nine years old, my cousin was assigned to the Air Force base in San Antonio, Texas. Because of the Walt Disney television show and the Davy Crockett phenomenon that was sweeping the country, I was a big Davy Crockett fan. My cousin sent me books on the Alamo and the history of the battle. I memorized all 181 Texans who died there. My fifth grade teacher told me it was useless information. "You should put more effort into your regular studies," she told me. She was right, of course. But even back then I put my efforts into what I liked—sports and history—and I looked for and studied the significant moments in each, hoping that some day, I'd make history, too.

When I can, I visit significant historical places while on my scouting trips. Growing up, I'd studied the Civil War, becoming fascinated with Gettysburg, and the Seven Days battle around Richmond, among other epic battles. When I grew up, I said to myself, I want to visit those historic sites. My family couldn't afford to travel to those places when I was young, so I read a lot of books. My first visits to a lot of historic sites happened in my imagination.

Sometimes I visit places by design, sometimes by whim. Usually, it depends if I have enough time while I'm driving from one town to another, from one scheduled interview to another. My trip to Oklahoma, Missouri, Nebraska, and Kansas in April 2005 was a little of both. I had flown into Lincoln, Nebraska, to attend a football camp, then driven to Kansas City to do some interviews. Along the way, I stopped in St. Joseph to spend 30 minutes walking through the Jesse James home, where the outlaw was shot to death about 125 years ago. After interviewing four prospects in Kansas City, I headed for Emporia.

Suddenly, I was struck by an idea that had come to me before, over the past few years, while driving through Kansas. I remembered a place I had always wanted to visit—the site of Knute Rockne's 1931 plane crash. After passing through Emporia, I noticed a small town called Bazaar. I had heard that name several times during my life, mostly from an uncle, who said it was the site of Knute Rockne's plane crash. I also had heard that there was a monument dedicated to the legendary Notre Dame coach, but it was in a remote and isolated area, very difficult to get to. On a whim, I turned off I-35 and onto Kansas route 50 and figured I'd give myself one hour to find the Rockne site. The sun would be down by 8:30 at night and I would be arriving in the Bazaar area between 7 and 7:30.

I stopped for gas in a very small town called Strong City and discovered I was already lost. It was 7:15, and I was just about to give up when fate intervened. At the gas station, I asked someone behind the counter if he knew where to find the Knute Rockne Memorial. No one in the gas station knew where it was; none of them even knew who Knute Rockne was. At that point, I decided to call off my search, since the sun would be down in an hour.

When I went to my car to pump gas, I thought I would ask one last person, a guy wearing a cowboy hat and driving a pickup truck. His name was Ed Koger. I asked him if he had heard of Knute Rockne. Yes, he said. In fact, Koger was born and raised in Bazaar. But he hadn't been back to his hometown in 30 years. He was on his way to his ranch in

Wichita. He added that he also knew about the Rockne Memorial, but wasn't exactly sure where it was. He said there was only one person still alive that actually had seen and heard the plane crash. But he said he had not seen that man in close to 30 years.

I thanked him for his time and was all set to drive back to I-35 before it got dark. But before I could go, Koger said that if I had time, I could follow him 20 miles south of Strong City and he would stop by the old house where the lone surviving witness used to live and see if he was still there. I quickly agreed.

We traveled 20 miles before we reached a town called Matfield Green, where there was only one house within sight. There was an old barn in the front of the property. We drove around on a small gravel road and came to a well-worn house with an old blue Chevy truck parked in front. We knocked on the front door but got no response. About a minute later, we heard some rattling by the back door. Out came a spry and very alert 88-year-old man who gave us a warm welcome. He immediately recognized my tour guide even though he hadn't seen him in three decades.

Arthur Conan Doyle once wrote through his alter ego, Sherlock Holmes, that if you were searching for Providence, you would find it in the flowers. Well, my proof of Providence came in the form of an 88-year-old man named Easter Heathman. After it was explained to him why we were there and what I was looking for, he said without hesitation, "We better get going because the sun is about to go down and, if it does, we will never find the Memorial in the dark." Easter must have taken hundreds of people to the site over the past 74 years.

We drove south in the old man's Chevy truck on Kansas route 177 for about two miles, then turned right off the road into the Kansas plains and into the year 1931. Earlier, Easter had laughed when I suggested that we use my rental car and I soon understood why. We had left the main road and were driving over bumpy and hilly terrain, following the tracks left by a farmer's pickup truck.

As we drove along, Easter told me the story of how, when he was 14 years old, he had witnessed a part of history, one of the biggest news stories of the early 1930s. It was March 31, just before 11 in the morning, when Easter heard a loud engine noise coming from the sky. It was a very cloudy day and he heard the engine circling but could not see the plane. He heard the noise for over a minute and then, all of a sudden, he heard the crash.

Getting to the spot was no easy task. Easter is a local celebrity and is one of very few people with keys to the many cattle fences surrounding this area. He walks with a cane because he broke his back three years ago. Just two weeks before I met him, he had fallen into the water while fishing and almost drowned. We stopped to open the gates of a few fences. Then we drove over one last hill and I could finally see the Rockne Memorial off in the distance. We got out of the truck about five minutes before the sun went down and Easter told me the rest of the story.

After hearing the plane crash, he ran to the spot and was one of the first people to view the national tragedy. At the time, he had no idea who Knute Rockne was. He said the sight of the eight bodies strewn around the accident site broke his heart. Easter then walked me around to the western edge of the site where there were several rocks lined up in a north-to-south fashion. He told me that he had placed those rocks there because it was the exact spot where he had found Knute Rockne's body. There had always been rumors that Rockne had been clutching a Rosary in his hand when his body was found. Easter confirmed those rumors as true. Interestingly, the memorial itself, a tall stone edifice, doesn't mention who Rockne was. It merely notes the names of the eight people who were killed on that day.

We stood there for close to a half-hour, just taking in the entire scene. There was an orange crescent glow in front of us as the sun went down and it gave the area an eerie look. Nowhere in sight—north, south, east, or west—could I see another living being, a road, or even a telephone pole, no sign of technological advancement since 1931. I'm not a believer in ghosts, or at least I've never really thought much about the subject, but with the wind whistling in my ears and with the eerie silence that prevailed, I couldn't help but feel that there were more than just the two of us present. For one brief moment, I heard quiet whispers in the wind. But Easter broke the silence and joked that this kind of atmosphere and time of day tends to lead people to some wild thoughts.

After saying a couple of prayers, I finally found something that Easter couldn't do—find the right button on my camera to take a quick snapshot of me standing next to the Memorial. Then I realized a little too late that the sun had gone down and we were standing in total darkness.

I couldn't thank Easter enough for his time and kindness to a perfect stranger. As I got back in my car and pointed it toward Wichita, I was excited and couldn't wait to tell people about my experience. I was amazed at the unusual circumstances that led me to find the Knute Rockne crash site. But even more so, I enjoyed the hour and a half I spent with a true American, a card-carrying member of the greatest generation, who went out of his way to make a lost recruiting analyst feel at home.

◆　　◆　　◆

If I had to list the most interesting people I've ever met, Easter would definitely be near the top. But if I could only list high school football players, I'm sure there would be a fair amount of players that most people have never heard of. Michael Oher and Jimmy Clausen certainly come to mind. But there are also lesser-known people I remember well, like Paul Glonek, an All-America lineman from Burbank, Illinois, that I met in the mid-1980s. He played on a team that produced at least eight Division I players. Glonek wasn't so stable. He signed with Notre Dame. A month later, the admissions office discovered a discrepancy in his test scores. They suspected that someone might have taken exams for him. So he was dropped. Later, Glonek's father drove his son to Illinois for an unofficial visit. When he arrived at Memorial Stadium in Champaign, coach Mike White and assistant Bill Callahan were waiting for him. Scott Davis, one of Illinois' top players and later a standout with the Oakland Raiders, sped by on his motorcycle. Glonek jumped on the back and they took off. White and Callahan didn't see much of him for the next few days.

Glonek signed with Illinois but he never made it to the fall. He spent two months in the school's summer bridge program and was penalized twice for damaging a dormitory room and stealing a pizza from a pizza deliveryman. Then he went to Iowa. He got into a fight with another Iowa player and broke his jaw, then left Iowa City after playing in only one game, a postseason bowl game. It cost him a year of eligibility. So he transferred to Arizona. He sat out one year, got involved in a restaurant brawl, played one season, was selected in the NFL draft, but didn't make it. It all adds up to an interesting story, but a lot of wasted talent. Glonek might have established an NCAA record by signing with four colleges.

I also found Chris Krause very interesting—he wasn't nearly as talented as Glonek, but he was an overachieving linebacker at North Chicago, Illinois, who chose Vanderbilt over Northwestern, Iowa State, and the Air Force Academy because they'd offered him a full scholarship and an opportunity to play in the football-crazy Southeastern Conference. He had a big heart and a lot of ambition. He wanted to stay in football, but he knew his limitations. He knew football wouldn't take him to the NFL. He realized quickly that he wasn't good enough to play professionally when he saw some of his All-SEC classmates get cut after being drafted by NFL teams. But he knew that football could help pay for his college education, something he couldn't afford by himself. More important than playing in the SEC, a diploma from Vanderbilt meant that he was being educated at one of the top 25 academic schools in the nation.

He majored in human organizational development, consulting for the business world. Krause wanted to get into sports training and physical therapy. His counselors recommended this curriculum. It was exactly what he needed, learning how to train and teach student-athletes to market themselves and empower themselves professionally, how to get to the next level. Through school, he met Preston Dennard, who once played for the Los Angeles Rams. Dennard owned a franchise in a recruiting company called College Prospects, which established itself in Chicago in 1989. But Krause wanted to expand on a bigger scale, not just Lake County in Illinois. He wanted to take advantage of the Internet and other resources. He wanted more than just sending a letter to a coach and hoping for a return.

In 2000, Krause launched National College Scouting Association, a Chicago-based firm with 25 full-time, in-house employees and 45 scouts around the country. Its database lists 40,000 college coaches in 30 sports and 1,700 colleges and universities in Division I, II, III, NAIA and Junior College. This year, NCSA has 10,000 clients. Krause says his mission is "to systematically match college coaches with qualified high school student-athletes through education and technology, build lasting relationships with college coaches, and ask questions that need to be answered."

It is a monumental task, but a very exciting one. Over the last 20 years, Chris and I have witnessed the same phenomenon in college sports. With recruiting limitations forced by Title IX legislation—including dramatic reductions in both scholarships in revenue sports and also the amount of time that recruiters can spend on the road—there is a bigger need for student-athletes to take a more active role in marketing themselves. NCSA helps to fill that need.

I think so much of what Chris is doing that I serve on NCSA's board of advisors. Of the thousands of boys and girls in the Class of 2005 who signed up for his service, 96 percent of them went on to play in college. And most participated in a sport other than football and basketball.

NCSA has uncovered some startling statistics about the recruiting process. According to the Big 10 Conference, over 50 percent of the kids who signed men's basketball scholarships in the 1990s either dropped out, flunked out, or transferred to another school by the end of their sophomore year. It's shocking, considering how difficult it is to get a scholarship in the first place. Only five percent of all students who participate in high school sports will go on to compete in college at some level, and only eight-tenths of one percent of those students will earn fully-funded Division I scholarships.

The chances are just too slim: players can no longer rely on luck, hoping that a college will discover them. Athletes and their parents must be involved in the recruiting process. Nobody can guarantee a scholarship—not NCSA or anyone else—but what Krause promises is a maximum of exposure, matching athletes with the highest probability of schools that fit their credentials. He reminds players that hundreds of schools are looking for qualified athletes, and that players don't have to attend a Division I school to get a great education.

Near Chris Krause on my list of interesting players would be Eugene Napoleon, who now runs a hip-hop record company in New Jersey. He was a very enterprising kid. He started to call me after his sophomore year. I had no idea if he had any talent. He was small, but I thought he had potential to be a Division I player because of his speed. He signed with Pittsburgh, but I felt he was being misused. I thought he was better than the player ahead of him. I talked to Illinois coach Mike White about him. White was looking for a running back. But Napoleon visited Illinois and didn't like it as much as West Virginia, and he eventually transferred there.

In 1988, he scored a touchdown for West Virginia during a game against Syracuse that was being televised by ESPN. While still in the end zone, he ran in front of a TV camera and shouted, "Hi, Tom Lemming." I was shocked to hear my name on national television, and that moment is probably what makes him one of the most memorable players I've known.

Still, hearing my name on national television isn't what convinced me that I'd finally made a place for myself in the scouting world. That moment had come many years earlier, in 1980, when I was invited to attend the *Daily News* All-Area football awards dinner. The event was held at the Como Inn, one of Chicago's landmark restaurants before it was torn down; it was built in 1921 and Al Capone ate spaghetti and lasagna and canoli there.

That night was significant for my career because it gave me my first exposure to college coaches whom I hadn't met on the road in those early years—coaches from Miami, UCLA, USC, Texas, and Boston College. The evening was more like a convention, providing a real who's who of the coaching profession. Big name coaches were normally in Chicago during that time of year to visit recruits. NCAA rules prohibited them from making contact with the prospects in attendance, so the coaches sat in a back room while enjoying their terrific Italian meals.

I was able to make a lot of contacts with coaches and players. There, in one confined space, at least 50 college coaches were sitting in a relaxed and comfortable atmosphere. I developed a lot of credibility with coaches once they knew what I was all about, after I met them at the Como Inn. The banquet had such renowned guest speakers as Lou Holtz, Bo Schembechler, Mike White, Earle Bruce, Lloyd Carr, and Hayden Fry. And in 1999, I joined their ranks when I was asked to speak.

Now I sponsor my own banquet. The idea was conceived when the *Chicago Sun-Times* stopped conducting its awards dinner in 2000. As soon as I learned that they weren't going to sponsor a banquet after 30 years of doing so, I wanted to organize a similar event. With my event, I wanted to recognize an All-Chicago Area team composed of prospects endorsed by college coaches. I also wanted to invite 15 of the top juniors. I also wanted to extend an open invitation to any college coach who wanted to attend. Like the previous banquets, I'd also ask a college coach to be guest speaker. To date, the list of speakers includes Iowa's Kirk Ferentz, Nebraska's Bill Callahan, Illinois' Ron Zook, and Notre Dame's Charlie Weis.

The event has gotten a great response. More than 30 colleges were represented at last year's banquet. For the players, it's a great way to meet assistant coaches, the ones who work in the trenches in recruiting. Of course, in accordance with NCAA rules, they can't mingle with the players, so they sit at the back of the room. But the players know they are there. Lots of business can be transacted in an atmosphere like that. For example, in 2004, Zook showed up at the banquet. He had recently been hired at Illinois and was actively recruiting assistant coaches to fill his staff. He hired Reggie Mitchell, who was then at Michigan State, and Curt Mallory, who was at Indiana, on the spot, right there at the banquet.

It costs about $7,000 to reserve the banquet hall and pay for the food and drinks for about 250 people. In the past, I used my own money to meet expenses, but recently I've had sponsors. One thing I don't have to pay for is a guest speaker; the coaches want to speak. Speaking in front of the top players in the Chicago area is a chance they can't pass up.

Two of the most interesting college coaches I have met are Nebraska's Bill Callahan and Michigan's Lloyd Carr. Callahan has an interest in almost everything, especially history and sports, which is part of why I found him so interesting. A one-time Chicagoan, he is also well versed in Chicago history. Similarly, when I met Lloyd Carr for the first time, I thought he was more like a college professor than a football coach. Recently, I was meeting Mike DeBord, Michigan's offensive coordinator, at a coffee shop in Ann Arbor. Carr heard about it, so he joined us. He was calm, with a smile always on his face, not at all like his sideline persona. He wanted to hear about my travel stories—what I've seen. Some coaches ask about those things but they don't really listen. They're just trying to be polite. But Lloyd Carr genuinely seemed to get a kick out of my travels.

Carr asked interesting questions, too. No matter where I'd been, he'd been there at some point as well. He has such a homespun way of talking that I immediately became disarmed and felt comfortable in his presence. I guess that's the key to his success. Players talk about the family atmosphere at Michigan more than any other program in the country.

Of course, with so many years and so many miles behind me, I'm bound to meet some interesting people who aren't involved with football. Some of the most memorable include legendary boxing champion Muhammad Ali, whom I met at a fundraising event. Ali walked in the room—gracious, funny, and warm—and I asked him to sign an autograph for my son Tommy. I've also met two world-class businessmen: Fred Smith, the founder and CEO of Federal Express, and Frank Eck, CEO of Advanced Drainage Systems, the largest drainage company in the world

Two years ago, former Akron coach Pete Cordelli called me and asked if I'd look at a quarterback who was the son of a friend of his. He felt the kid had big-time ability and he wanted to know what I thought. By the way, he told me, his father is Fred Smith of Federal Express. At the time, I didn't know who Fred Smith was. I told Cordelli that I wouldn't be in Memphis until March, to ask Fred Smith if his son could go to the San Antonio combine in January, that I could evaluate him then.

Cannon Smith turned out to be a talented and promising player, the best high school quarterback in Mississippi. He committed to Ole Miss. After the U.S. Army game, I met Fred Smith at the Alamo. It was then, for the first time, that I learned who he really was. He is a truly down-to-earth guy. I was mesmerized by his rags-to-riches story and his relationship with Elvis Presley. I like people in the Abraham Lincoln mold, people who have accomplished a lot but remain humble. I admire people like that.

Frank Eck has that same way about him. He's been calling me for 25 years. He loves to talk about football recruiting and the Chicago Cubs.   I didn't know who he was when he called the first time. Just another caller, I thought. But I finally pinpointed who he was, and I learned that he's donated nearly $100 million to Notre Dame—his alma mater—over the years. His name is on the university's law school, its baseball field, its indoor baseball practice facility, its tennis pavilion, and its bookstore quad. Still, he is a very unassuming gentleman.

But the most engaging and interesting person I have met along the recruiting trail is Jim Caviezel, the actor who has starred in 28 motion pictures, including *Thin Red Line*, *Wyatt Earp*, *Count of Monte Cristo*, and *Passion of the Christ*. Two years ago, he met Pete Schivarelli, manager of the rock group Chicago, at a concert in Los Angeles. Pete knew Caviezel was interested in football so he hooked him up with me.

I was at the Tennessee/Alabama game the first time Jim called me. He wanted to talk about football and religion, not movies. Jim called me frequently from his movie trailer in New Orleans, where he and Denzel Washington were working on *Déjà Vu*, the first movie to be filmed in the city after Hurricane Katrina. Caviezel is from Seattle, and is a University of Washington fan. His brother-in-law, Scott Linehan, was the offensive coordinator for the Miami Dolphins and is now the head coach of the St. Louis Rams. Though I was more interested in how they were filming the movie, Jim wanted to talk about a prospect he had heard was being recruited by Washington coach Tyrone Willingham.

Caviezel is Catholic and is one of the most spiritual people I've ever met. He has become somewhat of a spiritual adviser to me. I've never met anyone who knows so much about the Bible. Whenever I mention a verse, he finishes the line. Once, while he was staying in my home, he attended a local Catholic service, and he walked out because he thought the service was too progressive. He is a fascinating, intelligent guy who doesn't have a huge ego or an entourage.

A good part of my life is spent talking to football people, and many of them have been fascinating, but I also enjoy talking to people outside of the football world, from actors to men like Easter Heathman. I've collected so many memories—only some of which I've described here—that it would take a whole other book to fit them all into. So for now, I hope this chapter will do.

19

ADVICE TO ATHLETES

I ALWAYS ENCOURAGE PLAYERS to make educated decisions when it comes to selecting a college. That means not jumping at the first school to offer a scholarship. It means being patient and weighing all of your options. Players should compare schools, take campus visits, and gain as much knowledge about each school as possible. They need to look at not just the tradition of the football program and how many players the school has sent to the NFL, but at academics, curriculum, the makeup of the student body, tutoring, and the social environment.

A key to having a successful school visit—official or otherwise—is to strike out on your own and talk to second and third stringers about how well they are treated at the school. Remember, every school assigns their most personable and loyal players to show recruits around. You want to talk to every player at every level of the team to get a different and perhaps more objective view of the program. Find out what different players think of the coaching staff and the faculty and the school. Also, talk to non-athlete students about how the football players are perceived. Do your own questioning of people who aren't closely involved with the football program as opposed to just trusting the people who are escorting you around the campus. Circumvent all the hype, the puff, and the glitz that the coaches point out like so many tour guides. College players who show recruits around are told what to say. It isn't always an objective viewpoint. The trick is to get a better and more honest understanding of what the program has to offer.

This kind of investigation will help a player avoid the two thing recruits find most disheartening after a few months on campus: the depth chart and the opportunity to play early. A lot of recruits are led to believe they will play right away, then realize there is much more depth at the school at their position than they had been told. They discover, often to their utter surprise, that there is a pecking order much like in the military. The head coach is the general, the assistant coaches are the captains and lieutenants, and the players are the lowly buck privates. Talking to players currently in that situation while you visit can help you avoid this disappointment.

Impressionable prospects also are duped by the personalities of the assistant coaches who recruit them. During the recruiting process, an assistant coach becomes a recruit's best friend and has a lot of influence on a player's decision to attend one school or another. He talks to them like he is 18 years old, even though he might be much older. But once the recruits make a commitment and arrive on campus, they realize too late that there is no longer a bond between them and the person who recruited them.

When asked, I advise kids to wait and take their time. If a player is as good as coaches say he is, they will wait until he's ready to commit, after he's visited other schools and compared offers. If an athlete is heavily recruited and has a lot of options, he should wait until the end of the football season to see if his favorite head coach is still at the school of his choice. A lot of coaching changes are made at the end of the year. Sometimes, players commit early to a coach and a staff, only to see them gone come December. It doesn't make sense to commit to a school early and close out your recruiting, then be left out in the cold when the person who recruited you has been fired or has gone elsewhere.

But if a player is a borderline Division I prospect and is offered a scholarship, it might be best to commit early because he'll have fewer options than a blue-chipper. Generally, if it's early September of your senior year and you have only one or two offers, you should jump at one of them because there is no telling how long those offers will remain on the table.

By September, a big-time prospect typically has 10 to 50 offers. He can afford to make an educated decision and compare all the big schools and wait until he takes at least three of the five official visits that the NCAA allows. A good example was Drew Henson. He committed to Michigan before his junior year. He had a gentlemen's agreement with Michigan coach Lloyd Carr that Michigan wouldn't recruit another quarterback during his junior year or the year after. And they didn't. After three years at Michigan, Henson was a Heisman Trophy candidate. But he opted for baseball and signed with the New York Yankees.

Florida's Chris Leak also made a good decision. He learned a lot about recruiting by watching his older brother C.J. go through he process. C.J. had committed to Notre Dame, but on signing day he opted for Wake Forest because they'd promised to build their program around him, which didn't happen. C.J. transferred to Tennessee after his career stalled. He played, got hurt, and never fulfilled his potential. Because of that, Chris' father, Curtis, wanted to make sure that his youngest son would not face the same problems. Chris was leaning toward Tennessee because C.J. had transferred there. Over the next year, however, he and Curtis felt other schools would benefit him more, that others were more conducive to his style of play. Chris was rated as the No. 1 player in the country and could go wherever he wanted.

He narrowed his list to Florida, Florida State, Texas, USC, and Iowa. The Leaks felt Florida's Ron Zook was the most sincere head coach. He told Chris he would be the starting quarterback as a freshman. And it happened. Two years later, Zook was fired and went to Illinois, but Leak was named SEC freshman of the year and began to emerge as one of the most prolific quarterbacks in Florida history.

Curtis Leak did a flawless job of finding the right school for his son. If all parents were like him, there would be very few problems in college football recruiting. He learned from his previous mistakes with his older son and put together a picture-perfect recruiting plan for Chris. He let the schools battle each other while he sat back and determined in his mind which school would be best for his son's style. Of all the fathers I have dealt with over the years, Curtis Leak had the best plan.

Some players make good decisions because they are good people. For instance, Chris Zorich grew up in one of the worst neighborhoods on Chicago's South Side. He was an outstanding football player but he was only a borderline student. Yet he didn't put academics on the backburner. He was one of the most focused 18-year-olds I had ever met. He enrolled at Notre Dame. Today, he is a lawyer and runs the Chris Zorich Foundation and food pantry in Chicago.

John Foley also grew up in a tough neighborhood on Chicago's South Side, in a gang-infested area. He recalls shootings all the time as two street gangs, the Latin Kings and 26, fought for turf. One of five children, he got one pair of gym shoes a year and never owned a sport coat. But he remembers his family was never hungry, and the gangs never bothered him because he was a good athlete. He played on a grammar school football team that won 73 of 77 games in seven years. When St. Rita football coach Pat Cronin, a legendary figure in the neighborhood, came to his house for breakfast and offered a scholarship, John couldn't wait to put on a helmet and shoulder pads.

At St. Rita High School, he concentrated on football and virtually ignored his education. He was *USA Today's* defensive player of the year in 1985. But he scored 11 on his ACT exam.

Despite his low grades, Foley was recruited by nearly every major college. Some said he didn't have to study hard, that they'd take care of him, not to worry about staying eligible. But as the poster boy for the Chicago Catholic League, once tabbed as the most competitive high school football conference in the nation, it was a no-brainer for Foley to enroll at Notre Dame. He and Tony Rice became the only Proposition 48 players to be enrolled at the school. He was warned that he would have to work harder than ever if he hoped to graduate. But Foley honestly didn't think he would have to get a job after college. He figured he'd be in the NFL. Lou Holtz didn't feel the same way; he though Foley was too aggressive, that he wouldn't last four years, that he'd get hurt, that he would be happy to get two years out of him. But Holtz did guarantee Foley that he would get a good education and have a good job when he graduated.

Foley sat out one year, had an outstanding sophomore season, and was projected as an All-American as a junior. But then he suffered a career-ending neck injury while blocking for Tim Brown on a kickoff in the last game of his sophomore year against Texas A&M. After his injury, Foley discovered that even friends were betting that he would flunk out, that he'd end up being a beer truck driver like his father. He was devastated. He thought he was invincible and found out the hard way that he wasn't. He went through severe depression, asking himself, "What am I going to do? What will I do if I can't play football?"

While at Notre Dame, Foley learned that he suffered from dyslexia. He didn't even know what it was. But it explained why he had so much trouble reading, why he was so embarrassed when asked to read in front of his classmates in high school and why he tested so poorly. It was a relief to finally figure out what was wrong, and that's when his education took off. Foley went to see a psychiatrist at Notre Dame who gave him a copy of Norman Vincent Peale's best-selling book, *Power of Positive*

Thinking. The book changed his life. He still gives copies to friends when they are experiencing difficult times.

Because of his willingness to work academically, Foley is a millionaire today, and he didn't do it through football. For the last eight years, John has been a turnaround specialist. He and his four-member team go into a financial company that is doing poorly, evaluate the situation, interview employees, and then write up a business plan. In his last two turnarounds, Foley saw the revenues of one investment company go from $1.5 million to $8 million in three years, and another company improve from $80,000 to $3.6 million in just over two years. Today, Foley, who is 39 years old, recalls the way it was when he was 19. He credits his mentors at Notre Dame—Frank Eck, Michael Roche, and Bob Takazawa—for the success he has achieved after football. And he thanks coach Lou Holtz, who stood by him and supported him after his injury. Without them, he says, he would be nowhere.

But some players make bad decisions because they don't take academics seriously or they take bad advice or fall in with people who lead them astray. That's what happened to Hubert "Boo Boo" Thompson of Proviso West High School in Hillside, Illinois. He was one of the best defensive linemen ever to come out of the Chicago area and a state heavyweight wrestling champion. He signed with Michigan State but had to sit out for two years because of poor grades. When Thompson became eligible, he played very well in his first and only year of college eligibility. Then, against everyone's advice, he opted for the NFL draft. It was a mistake. He needed more seasoning. He would have been a first-round NFL draft choice if he had stayed in school for two more years. Today, he is undergoing psychiatric evaluation after being charged with manslaughter.

The most tragic case of all is Philip Macklin of Proviso East High School in Maywood, Illinois. He was the *Chicago Sun-Times'* player of the year in 1998. A 6-2, 220-pounder, he could play any position. Without a doubt, he would be a star in the

NFL at 26—if he had gone to class and stayed out of trouble. But he fell in with the wrong crowd. And he didn't have good study habits. He signed with Illinois, but he couldn't get through the school's bridge program and went to a prep school, then attended two junior colleges. He was an All-American at Harper College in Palatine, Illinois, in 2001. In 2002, he and two roommates at Joliet Junior College were accused of holding up a clerk at a gas station and were sentenced to six years and six months in jail. Macklin was paroled in July 2005. Today, Macklin is in prison for the second time. In September 2006, he was indicted for armed robberies of two convenience stories. He faces a minimum of 21 years in prison. He had persuaded two 15-year-olds to commit the crimes and had provided them with a gun.

Imagine how good Macklin could have been. He should be in the middle of a great career in the NFL. Instead, it's probably the greatest waste of talent in Illinois football in the last 30 years. But at the very least, it's an example of how thoughtful you need to be when picking a school. Players making big decisions about their futures must remember that the passage from high school to college means they have become young adults. It is time to knuckle down and do the work necessary to have success in the next four years. It is a privilege to play college football, not a right. It comes down to the simplest advice: don't blow it.

20

ADVICE TO COACHES

THE BEST AND SIMPLEST PIECE OF ADVICE I can give to any high school coach is this: help your player get to college. That's the least a coach can do for a student who has dedicated four years of his life to a football program. If he is good enough, help him find a level of college competition where he can be competitive and enjoy the experience.

Some high school coaches claim it isn't in their job description to be involved in the recruiting process. I know it's hard work, cutting and mailing film, taking calls and spending time with college coaches. It is time consuming and arguably above and beyond what they are paid to do as coaches. It's true that recruiting isn't in their job description, but it ought to be. With thousands of scholarships available from Division I and II schools, and with forms of financial aid available for athletes in Division III, it's just irresponsible of coaches to avoid getting involved.

Because of NCAA rules, college coaches can't respond to a parent who mails a tape of his son, which makes it even more important for high school coaches to assist in the recruiting process. Colleges can look at tapes sent by coaches, and they will provide an objective evaluation to a high school coach. A well-informed high school coach can be worth his weight in gold in helping his players obtain scholarships. All things being equal, many grants-in-aid go to players whose coaches are more persuasive, who promote their players, who go out of their way to make the colleges aware of them.

For a coach, the most critical step in this process is determining at what level a student can play. Having a realistic idea of a player's capabilities helps coaches contact the right schools. One way to get a better idea of a player's skill level is to copy a lot of game film early on, then put together a highlight film and a game film and mail it to several area colleges and ask for feedback. Area colleges will almost always provide this service for films that come from high school coaches because they want to maintain good relationships; there's always the chance a coach could have a blue-chipper in the next year or two.

College coaches will provide honest appraisals. From there, the high school coach will know in which direction to proceed, to which level he should guide his player. Normally, the last several hundred scholarships will go to players represented by the most persuasive high school coaches because, at that point, players have similar skill levels. It's their coaches that help them stand out. For example, Coach Ted Ginn Sr. of Glenville High School in Cleveland, Ohio, goes on an annual weeklong caravan with members of his squad and players from other local schools to visit Big Ten and Mid-America Conference schools. Ginn introduces the players to college coaches and makes them aware of each player. College coaches respect Ginn because of his track record of sending players to Division I schools, including his son Ted Jr., the All-America wide receiver who went to Ohio State. The trip is a stroke of genius, providing great exposure for his players.

A high school coach should never hold back mail addressed to players. Some high school coaches prefer to wait until after the season to distribute mail. But colleges need to know right away if a player is interested; they need to make determinations as quickly as possible. If a coach is holding back mail, the end of the season might be too late. For example, a well-known coach in the Midwest once made a practice of withholding mail addressed to his players from college recruiters until after the season, which usually meant late November or early December. He was unaware that unless the player was a blue-chipper, colleges wouldn't come back to recruit him because they already had reached their maximum allotment of offers. So the coach lost a lot of scholarships for borderline players. He apparently didn't understand that colleges will wait until hell freezes over for a great player, but not for borderline ones—there are already so many of them on their list. The coach was unaware that he was hurting his players' chances to go to college. Finally, some parents alerted him to the situation, and the coach adjusted; now he distributes the mail and allows his players to get phone calls during the season. And today, his players receive scholarship offers earlier than ever before.

In holding back mail, I don't think coaches are intentionally trying to hurt their players. Some coaches are just unaware of all the changes that have occurred in the recruiting process in the last 10 years. They don't know that a majority of scholarships are offered by the end of June, before a prospect's senior year even begins. So high school coaches should be sure to distribute all mail to kids as soon as possible. He also should be sure that colleges have players' phone numbers and email addresses. That way, a player has a fighting chance to obtain a college scholarship.

I also believe coaches should be aware of combines, which are designed to help expose a player's skills to college recruiters. Some combines are better than others. There are combines sponsored by shoe companies, recruiting services, colleges, and independents. A coach must determine if a particular combine will benefit his player. Combines are valuable to players who need exposure and need to make a name for themselves. But great players don't have to go; combines can even hurt a really great player's chances for a scholarship if he attends but doesn't perform well. For example, if a player runs a 4.7 at a combine when he's run a 4.4 in the past, his evaluation will take a nosedive in the eyes of the college recruiters. That player could quickly drop from a 4-star prospect to a 3-star in the click of a stopwatch. In my view, it makes absolutely no sense for a blue-chipper to attend a combine; he's already ranked at the top of his position and can only go down in someone's estimation. But for borderline players, combines can make all the difference.

Coaches should also be aware of camps that pressure players into coming by telling them that they won't be rated high or won't be considered as an All-American if they don't attend. Those camps are only out to make money, and coaches need to help their players choose a combine for the right reasons.

This may seem obvious, but players need to be able to rely on coaches for sound advice. Gary Korhonen of Richards High School in Oak Lawn, Illinois, is another good example of what a coach can do to help his players. In 34 years at Richards, Korhonen has known great success. He produced undefeated state championship teams in 1988 and 1989 and finished second in 2001. He has won more than 300 games in his career and recently became the winningest football coach in Illinois history. But he is most proud of the number of players he has sent to college: 86 to Division I schools; 53 to Division II; 83 to Division III; and 41 to junior colleges.

Korhonen is a terrific salesman. He mails film to college coaches before they come to Chicago. He makes the time to talk about his players, and he always puts them in a positive light. He will call sportswriters, recruiting analysts, colleges— whoever can help get one of his players a scholarship. He always sends me tapes early on and I put his players in my magazine. He also produces profiles for his players, complete with statistics and academic history. During the May evaluation period, he is prepared for anyone who walks in the door to ask about any of his players. Because of his exuberance, all other things being equal, his players are often taken ahead of others because, thanks to his hard work, college recruiters are more familiar with them.

Every year, Korhonen tries to get at least half a dozen players into college at some level. It is up to the college coaches to turn him down. That's why so many parents are happy with the way he does things.

Another high school coach who does an excellent job with recruiting is Bill McGregor of DeMatha in Hyattsville, Maryland. McGregor does a great job of getting full scholarships for his kids, sometimes as many as 20 in one year. McGregor is part of his own recruiting service. He contacts schools and often cajoles college coaches into taking kids of lesser talent with the idea that better prospects are coming in a year or two. He uses his blue-chip players to help attract scholarships for borderline players. College coaches respect McGregor, whose football program is dominant year after year.

Another exemplary high school coach is George Smith of Fort Lauderdale Aquinas, in Fort Lauderdale, Florida. Smith, who sent Michael Irvin to Miami and the NFL and freshman tackle Sam Young to Notre Dame, is the best coach in Florida when it comes to getting scholarships for his players. He has developed an interesting tactic for showing off his players: instead of participating in combines—something he doesn't like his players to do—his players get exposure from workouts and jamborees Smith schedules specifically for college coaches to attend. I've never heard a negative thing said about him. He is tough, but also straight and to the point.

Then there's Russ Probst of Hoover High School in Birmingham, Alabama. Probst is an outstanding self-promoter, a P.T. Barnum for teenagers. His program receives national exposure with *Two-a-Days*, a made-for-teens cable television show that serializes his team ala *Laguna Beach*. He isn't afraid to schedule any opponent. His team has traveled to Ohio, Arkansas, and Oklahoma to play games against other nationally rated teams. He gives his players a lot of exposure, and they love him for it.

High school coaches all over the country can learn from these coaches, coming up with their own ways to promote their players. The effort a coach puts forth on a player's behalf could make a big impact on that player's future. That's something no coach should take lightly, no matter what the official job description.

21

ADVICE TO PARENTS

I ONCE DID A ROUNDTABLE DISCUSSION for my CSTV show with former Super Bowl MVP Phil Simms, his son Matt, and Matt's football coach, Greg Toal. Matt was ranked as the No. 60 player in the nation, one of the top nine quarterbacks. I asked Phil, "How involved will you be in the recruiting of your son?"

He said, "I learned my lesson with my older son Chris [a former Texas quarterback who now plays for the Tampa Bay Buccaneers]. I didn't get involved with his recruiting. He wanted to handle it and I allowed him to do most of it." Chris first committed to Tennessee, then switched to Texas at the last minute. At Texas, he got into a battle for the starting quarterback position with Major Applewhite, and so never fully realized his potential in college.

"Every parent should be involved in their son's decision," Phil said. "After all, they are only 17 years old. They aren't adults, despite what they think. Parents have the best interests of their son in mind. They should be involved in the decision because their son isn't mature enough to make that important a decision on his own."

Phil Simms is absolutely right. Parents have to take charge of recruiting or the consequences can be devastating. College coaches have their own best interests in mind, so parents have to be the ones looking out for their child's best interests. Parents should be privy to conversations between the coach and their son, what is being talked about, so they aren't taken by surprise. Although parents shouldn't be so dominating as to just decide for their child, they must be sure to point him in the right direction, encouraging him to make a good decision for the right reasons. Don't ever let your son make his college decision on his own.

I strongly recommend that parents go on official visits with their sons. I say this for several important reasons. Adults usually have a better, more balanced view of the school, whereas 17-year-olds don't have the same kind of perspective and tend to focus on less important things, like girls or parties. School officials will present more information about academics if parents are there. Most importantly, if parents allow their child to go on a visit alone, the trip could turn out to be little more than 48 hours of partying with players on the team.

Don't think that a crazy, drunken visit isn't usually the case. There are hundreds of stories every year about the organized debauchery going on. A recruit from Chicago told me that he and another Chicago player went on an official visit to a Big Ten school and both got dead-solid drunk for the first time in their lives. One player vomited in the hood of the other player's sweatshirt and was so sick that he couldn't attend the breakfast meeting the next day. A player from Chicago visited an SEC school. The coach who was recruiting him said there would be a lot of pretty girls waiting for him when he arrived at the school. He spent 48 hours partying and drinking with girls. He experienced two huge hangovers. When it was time to leave for home on Sunday, a graduate assistant and some girls took him to the airport. One of them referred to the business school as they drove by it, saying only, "Oh, there it is." The prospect left the campus without really seeing the business school, which had been one of the things he'd told his parents he'd wanted to look at.

Sadly, if a player has a good enough time at a school—even if they spent most of that time drunk—they come home wanting to go there more than before. For example, another player went on a visit to a Big Ten school and fell in love with one of the escorts and committed to the school because of the girl. He didn't realize she was a senior. He talked to her on the phone for the next couple of months and signed with the school. But she graduated and left the school before he enrolled. He was heartbroken, and he was also stuck at a school for the wrong reasons. That's why parental involvement is so critical. Remember, choosing the right college is the most important decision in your son's life up to this point. You want to be sure he is in a comfortable environment so he can grow athletically and academically.

Something I've learned over the past three decades is that a majority of recruits will tell parents what they want to hear when it comes to their own priorities. The truth is, most recruits are more interested in finding the quickest route to the NFL. I remember one of the nation's top prospects needed to attend a school that offered a special program to take care of his needs because he suffered from attention deficit disorder. But he was recruited nationally, and not all schools offer such programs. He visited one southern school and players took him to a strip club, where he drank a lot of alcohol. He got so drunk that he got sick and had trouble getting home on the plane. His father was furious that the school had taken his son, who was underage and had never had a drop off alcohol before, to a strip joint and gotten him drunk. He called the school and asked, "How can you do this to my son?" The coach said, "All schools are doing it." Eventually, the father took the bull by the horns and made sure that his son went to a school that offered a special program for him.

Remember, it is tougher for football players to deal with college life than for typical students. Because they have to find time to study while making time for film sessions, practice, weight training, meetings, and games, their time is very limited. At party schools, the first thing that is cut from the priority list is academics. Party schools accommodate players by offering easy courses so their commitment to football won't be jeopardized and they'll remain eligible. Parents need to make sure that their child chooses a program where the coaches believe that players are students first, where coaches try to keep players' schedules academically oriented.

Just as assistant coaches have the magic to woo recruits with their friendly demeanors, they use the same tactics on parents. Keep in mind that the assistant coach is being paid to befriend you. A good recruiter can make his school sound like paradise: the best academic school, the best football school, the best party school—whatever it is a player (or his parents) is looking for. It is up to parents to bring their son down to earth and make him aware that maybe the school can't deliver on its promises.

Sometimes, parents are overwhelmed by a famous coach sitting in their living room. In such cases, they often forget to ask the proper questions that sometimes he wants to avoid. It is good to put a coach on the defensive with inquisitive and smart questions. Here are some examples of the kinds of questions parents need to ask, no matter how uncomfortable or rude it might seem:

How many football players do you graduate?

How many of those that graduate are minorities?

What kind of academic degrees are these players graduating with?

Are you tutoring players to be eligible or to earn worthwhile degrees?

Who watches over my son while he is on your campus?

Are the coaches close to the players?

Where do you want him to play?

Where do you expect him to play?

When do you want him to play?

How long will it take for him to get into the starting lineup?

Is he someone you're recruiting to be a starter or are you hoping to sign him to keep him away from your competition?

Are any current team members involved in any trouble, academic or otherwise?

Have some broken the law or been arrested?

How many current players are in danger of flunking out? How do you help them?

Write down the answers, or record them. Two or three years from now, you might find yourself happy to have documented such a conversation. And remember, football is only part of your son's college experience. Ask questions about academics and social life on campus. The coach should know these answers. If you can, talk to other players on the squad, not just the escorts who were handpicked by the head coach to show your son around the campus on his official visit. Ask them how they perceive the coaches and the program.

Of course, as a parent, it's important to have the right advice long before college recruiters come knocking at your door. First of all, parents need to understand that college coaches project how they think a recruit will perform at the college level. This isn't a new philosophy. It has been the primary focus of college recruiters for years. Unfortunately, many parents do not understand that colleges recruit on potential as much as they do on performance, sometimes even more so. When parents call me for advice, it is too late if their son is a senior. If they call during his junior year or before, the first thing I advise them to do is enroll their son in a speed camp. Speed is the most important thing to most recruiters. You can't do anything about size, and strength will come with time. But you can improve your chances in the recruiting process by reducing your time in the 40-yard dash.

Another thing parents can encourage their children to do is to learn to play multiple positions on offense and defense. It's helped many students land scholarships. Santino Panico of Libertyville, Illinois, played defense as a sophomore and offense as a junior. I advised him to play both as a senior, which he did. He ended up earning a scholarship to Nebraska, starting as a freshman as their kick returner.

Playing multiple positions also paid off for Tom Zbikowski of Buffalo Grove, Illinois. He was the player of the year in the Chicago area as a senior, a running quarterback. But he also played safety and returned kicks to show off his 10.5-second speed for 100 meters. In the end, he received more scholarship offers to play defensive back than quarterback even though he played defense for only one year in high school. The decision to try out other positions paid off; he played for Notre Dame and was an All-American last year. He figures to go on to play defense in the NFL.

Of course, you don't play football in high school to prepare for the NFL. You play where your coach needs you. I understand that. But if your son is playing a position that he won't be recruited for in college, I suggest that he try to play as many positions as possible on offense and defense and also return kicks to expose his athletic ability to college recruiters. If the coach can't offer those opportunities, there are other ways you can try. Take Garrett Seeger of Barrington, Illinois, as an example. I suggested to Seeger's father that Garrett should go to summer camps as a safety and talk to his high school coach about playing defense because his best opportunity to get a college scholarship was as a safety. But the coach felt Garrett was too valuable at quarterback. So Seeger went to Colorado's camp and offensive coordinator Shawn Watson said Seeger was the best free safety there. Seeger ended up as a safety at Boston College. This is just another way a player can use camps and combines to his recruiting advantage.

Unfortunately, too many parents don't take charge of their son's recruiting, which leaves him vulnerable to shady coaches. A majority of parents have never been in this situation before, so they trust the coaches. They relinquish responsibility for a decision that they should be involved in. Rather than sound stupid, parents exchange pleasantries with coaches and ignore the issues simply because they don't know the right questions to ask. But being thoughtful and prepared as you enter this process with your child goes a long way toward keeping yourself out of a bad situation.

As a parent, you have a right to be involved. Hopefully, I've provided some advice that will help you assert that right.

22

THE MAN BEHIND THE RANKINGS

AFTER ENROLLING IN FIRST GRADE at Our Lady of Good Counsel in Chicago, near 35th and Ashland, I had a few traumatic experiences. One of the most traumatic ones happened one day when I forgot my homework. I had already walked five blocks to school and made it to the playground when I realized I'd left my homework behind. I ran back home in a panic. In fear of what the nuns might do if I didn't make it back on time, I wet my pants. I got back to school and the nuns saw my pants. I had to take them off, wash them in a utility room in the basement, and wrap myself in a towel. Then I had to sit in class with the towel wrapped around my waist, waiting for my pants to dry. All the other kids were looking at me. It was the most embarrassing and humiliating experience of my childhood. I couldn't bear to tell my parents. I was only six years old at the time, but I remember it to this day. I can laugh about it now, but it was a very traumatic experience at the time.

I grew up Catholic, but I was scared to death of religion early on. Nuns had tried to change me from being left-handed to being right-handed. My older sister came home with horror stories of how the nuns beat boys with rulers. Ironically, we were a very Catholic family. My aunt was a cloistered nun and my cousin was a priest. My father was Irish-Catholic, a war hero with four bronze star medals. He was one of six children. He was an alter boy growing up and went to Mass every day before the war. While overseas, he drove an ammunition truck in North Africa and Italy. He was wounded in Italy, sent home in 1944 to recover, then was shipped back. After the war, he never lost faith in God, but he'd lost faith in religion. He only went to Mass on Christmas and Easter. It infuriated his family. He had a picture of Jesus and a rosary in his bedroom but I never saw him use them.

He was in his 40s when I was born. I hardly knew my father, who worked two jobs his whole life. He was a heavy-drinking Irishman. But he had a great sense of humor. One day, when I was eight, after a nun had told me in catechism class that if I missed church, I would go to hell, I ran into my father's room and told him he was going to hell if he didn't go to church on Sunday. He told me, "If you don't leave me alone, you'll be the one greeting me when I get there."

We moved to 48th and Lockwood after first grade and my parents couldn't afford to send me to Catholic school anymore. So I went to Sahs Elementary School for second grade in 1961. I had to leave school at one o'clock every Wednesday to go to catechism classes from one to four at Our Lady of Snows at 48th and Laramie.

In high school, I wasn't a straight-A student, so I couldn't get an academic scholarship. And I had no money for tuition. I had planned to attend Western Illinois, but I went to Europe instead. I had just enough money to get overseas, having saved from working two jobs, but it wasn't enough to live in quality. I slept in cheap hotels and youth hostels. I recall sleeping on the floor of a hotel in Amsterdam. I learned about World War II in London, the French Revolution in Paris, and the battle of Stalingrad in what is now Leningrad. I stayed in a grand hotel that Adolph Hitler was going to use when he conquered Stalingrad. Under a glass in front of the hotel is a card the Nazis had made up to invite people to a grand gala to celebrate their victory over Soviet Russia. It was the only time

I slept in a bed with a canopy. I've been to the pyramids in Egypt, the Vatican and Colosseum in Rome, the Acropolis in Greece, and I've spent a full day inside the Kremlin in Moscow during the Communist era. I've also visited Gorky Park, Lenin's Tomb, and St. Basil's Church in Red Square.

I received an education during my two years of traveling, but it wasn't one I could bank on. If I could do it all over again, I would have gone to college. I would have studied World or American history. Maybe I could have become a teacher. I think I could have been a good one, especially in a subject I love.

College could have helped me make contacts that could have bankrolled me to start my recruiting business in 1978 and 1979. Instead, because of a lack of funds, I found myself sleeping in my car and stapling 12 pages of information together and calling it a magazine. But I don't regret sleeping in my car or scrimping or saving. It was an adventure more than a hardship. I don't regret the thousands of people I met along the way.

Eventually, I married and started a family, but in 1993, we divorced after nine years of marriage. Our son, Tommy, was seven at the time. My ex-wife moved to Tampa, Florida, to teach at a Catholic school. Tommy lived with her for 10 years, but I saw him during the summer and whenever he wasn't in school. He even traveled with me from 1990 to 2001. Today, he is 20 years old and he lives with me in suburban Chicago. He has attended DePaul University in Chicago and plans to major in hotel management. He hopes eventually to run a restaurant or play guitar in a band.

I spend more time with Tommy than most divorced fathers do with their sons. When he was little, I never left him with a babysitter. He even went along with me on dates. For the 10 years before he graduated from high school and came to live with me, I spent June, July, and August and two weeks at Christmas with him. Unlike many divorces, where there is a lot of anger over children, we have never had a problem over

Tommy's upbringing. He was well grounded and disciplined. He was always the most important thing in both of our minds and still is, even though his mother has remarried and moved to San Jose, California. I even have a good relationship with Tommy's stepfather.

I started to take Tommy on trips when he was three. I paid him a couple of dollars a day to hand out clipboards and pens to players during interview sessions. It was good bonding. When he came along, I didn't drive for 18 hours a day. Instead, we did a lot of father-son things together. We went to Six Flags amusement parks across the country. We drove through a zoo near Ardmore, Oklahoma, where animals come right up to your car to be fed.

He never took to football at the time. He preferred video games and cars. But he had an opportunity to meet some of the great football players of this era—Peyton Manning, Randy Moss, Charles Woodson, Ahmad Green—while I was doing television shows at Disney World in Orlando, Florida. Disney World became our home away from home; we went there at least three times a year. We also enjoyed visiting Ghost Town in the Sky near Gatlinburg, Tennessee, Maggie Valley amusement park, and a Cherokee Indiana reservation in the Great Smoky Mountains.

We've spent a lot of time in Washington, D.C. We've visited the Capitol, Ford's Theatre, and taken all the tours at the Smithsonian Museum. One time, when we were in Dallas, we drove the exact route that President Kennedy took when he was assassinated. I like to give Tommy a sense of history. We've been to Gettysburg and Monticello. On my trips with Tommy, I take a few hours off every few days to do something together. We don't fish or surf or play golf. We just jog and walk and lift weights.

Now, travel-wise, I'm in more of a bind. My leisure time is reduced more than ever because I have to look for juniors earlier than ever before. There is no down time left in the recruiting process, no time to golf or fish or hunt or visit the

Grand Canyon. But there are still plenty of places in the world I want to see. If I had the time, I'd visit Israel. I would like to spend two months there, walking the steps that Jesus walked. I would like to get baptized in the Jordan River, where Jesus was baptized. I also want to visit Jordan and the ancient city of Petra. I've also never been to the Great Wall of China or Machu Picchu. I've been to Peru but never climbed the Andes to Machu Picchu, the Incas' great city in the sky.

While I'm on the road here in the states, I stop at different kinds of churches, mainly Christian. But a couple of times I have attended a Jewish temple, once in New York City and another time in Los Angeles, just to get a feel for the worship. No matter what church I'm at, I feel like all eyes are on me. It's not that I'm paranoid; it's just that I'm usually the only one wearing jeans, a t-shirt, and gym shoes, while the rest of the congregation is dressed in their Sunday finest. That is why I always sit in the back and make as little noise as possible. To me, it is fascinating to see how different services are run, particularly in the same religion. Every part of the country has its own significant way of preaching the gospel. I never leave a worship service until after the offering has been taken because I don't want to look like a deadbeat.

Six years ago, a friend, Christine Burkhardt, brought me to Willow Creek in my own neighborhood. It's a non-denominational church that embraces everyone, no matter who you are. I feel comfortable there. When I'm not on the road, I attend services every Wednesday night and Sunday morning.

Religion is important in football, too. Most teams pray together. Coaches, especially when they are recruiting Christians, use religion to their advantage. They start talking like evangelists. They bring up the name of the Lord in their recruiting message when visiting a recruit's home. For some coaches, Jesus is their best recruiter.

I helped bring the Christian network to the U.S. Army game. At times, I ask kids to organize Bible studies. People have told me that I should be more prominent in pushing people to the Lord because I am in a position of influence. But I don't feel comfortable doing it because, as a Christian, I shouldn't push and browbeat people from other religions to Christianity. But I do try, when given the chance, to push Christian kids closer to the Lord and their religion. I talk to football players about spiritual issues if, during our conversation, they bring up the Lord.

Overall, I feel my life so far has been a great journey that has only reached the halfway point. I've driven about 1.5 million miles on this journey, but I still have a long way to go. I figure I'll keep doing this for 25 to 30 more years, as long as I stay healthy. I want to be doing this job until I'm 75 or 80—that's how much I enjoy what I do. But I know eventually someone will have to follow in my footsteps, and I can only say that that person should have a pure love for football and recruiting. They can't think about money first. It took me seven years to make a profit in this business. It never was my first goal to get rich. I loved travel and history and football—that's what got me started.

A lot of recruiting analysts tell me that they are disappointed if they don't make money in the first year. There are about 500 of them out there, analyzing high school players in their areas of the country, four for every Division I school. All of them want to become rich right away. I tell them that if they have a love for the business and are willing to take time and put in a major effort, they will be successful. I couldn't afford to publish a quality magazine when I was starting out. Now, I believe it is a first-rate magazine.

Evaluating high school athletes isn't an exact science, any more than forecasting the weather or handicapping horses. It's an ongoing process. I always feel I can do better. Getting better comes with experience. And I've only been in this business for 28 years. Only God knows how much more growing there's left for me to do.

◆ ◆ ◆

Up until February 4, 2007, my job meant everything to me. But the events of that fateful day made me realize that there is more to life than working and recruiting.

It was Super Bowl Sunday. I left my house in the Chicago area at 1 o'clock in the morning after checking the Weather Channel, which informed me that I was to have clear driving all the way to my destination of Rochester, New York. Interstate 90 is only a mile from my home and it would take me all the way to Rochester without a detour. I was hoping to get to my hotel by 7:30 that evening so I could watch the Bears play the Colts.

Everything went smoothly in the beginning. I had no trouble as I passed through Toledo and Cleveland. But once I got to Erie, Pennsylvania, I noticed strong winds and dark clouds. Still, there was no snow yet. Once I crossed the Pennsylvania/New York state line and approached the toll road, the toll collector informed me that the Interstate was going to be closed at the next exit. I had to get off either there or at the next exit and seek shelter.

I had just gotten a call from Chris Lawlor of *USA Today*. He had been watching the Weather Channel and had noticed a major storm coming off of Lake Erie. He said I should get off I-90, go back 20 miles to I-86 and go through the southern part of New York. It would take longer but I'd be safe. He cautioned me, "Don't mess with the storms coming off Lake Eric. They can be killers."

I didn't listen to him; I wanted to save a few hours. So I continued on I-90. It was closed at the next exit, which was Westfield, New York. State troopers told me to take shelter. But I hadn't seen any snow yet. The only smart thing I did at the time was fill up with gas.

Then I made what could have been a fatal mistake. I got off I-90 and, instead of listening to anyone, got on Route 20, which unbeknownst to me went under I-90 and started to parallel Lake Erie. I headed north and the snow began to fall at an intensity that I had never seen before. Being from Chicago, I thought I had seen big snowstorms, but nothing matched what I saw that day.

I drove about 20 miles north to a town called Dunkirk. The snow continued to build up. I became disoriented. All road signs were covered with blowing snow. I left Route 20 and wound up on a little-used, narrow rural road that I later learned was Route 5. After driving for 20-25 miles, I noticed the snow was rising above my fender and I began to slow down. I was having trouble seeing the road even though there was still daylight.

When the snow reached the hood of my car, I stopped in the middle of the road. I couldn't be sure where the road was. I worried that if I had gone off the road with a white Taurus, nobody would ever find me in the snow. I put on my warning lights and sat there. I tried to keep from panicking. There was no one around. I was deep in a forest and the sun was going down and the snow was still coming down at an intense rate. I realized my blunder—sometimes my bullheadedness prevents me from listening to good advice from informed people—could cost me my life.

I sat there, waiting and praying, for five hours. The car got completely covered with snow. My only hope was that if someone came from behind me, they would see the blinking lights. I began to get calls from friends who wanted to talk football. They became concerned for my welfare once I told them where I was and what was going on.

Anthony Panico, who had contacts in New York, tried to call people to piece together a picture of my approximate location. Jim Caviezel, the actor, prayed with me for a while. And Rick Doering, a board member of my church, informed me that the storm had subsided about 40 miles north of my location. If I could get 40 miles north, I would be safe, he assured me.

I called my son Tommy to tell him that I loved him, that I was in a tough situation. I informed him where my finances were. I called my brother Terry, a lieutenant in the Illinois State Police. He called the New York State Police. But they told him that they couldn't get to me. They were too busy with accidents and overturned trucks and other problems created by the storm.

I decided to walk. It was the biggest gamble of my life. I could have stayed in the car, which had a full tank of gas. But I remembered seeing a gas station off the road a few miles behind me. Just getting out of the car took a great effort. I finally pushed aside the snow and got the door open. The wind was so fierce, and the snow was coming from the West at such a severe rate, that when I got out of my car, I lost my breath immediately.

I started walking, wearing only a fall jacket, a baseball cap, and trail boots. I didn't have any gloves. The snow was already thigh-high. It was dark now, and the cold kept slapping me in the face. Soon, I had no feeling in my feet, hands, or face.

Eventually, after about two miles, I saw a bank of lights. It was the gas station that I had seen hours before. It really lifted my heart. The gas station was full of people who also had been stranded. They stared at me. I must have looked like the abominable snowman. It took me a few hours to thaw out.

I hadn't eaten all day, so I stood in line to get a sandwich. I also bought a brush to sweep the snow off of my car. People there said they expected 12 feet of snow by the end of the week. I began to wonder how long I was going to be there. The whole idea of this trip was for me to get to New York City by February 7 to do five hours of live television programming on CSTV on national signing day. Now it looked like I was going to miss the whole show.

While waiting, I began to notice that every hour or so a big 18-wheel truck would slowly go past on Route 20. I decided that I would go out and hail the next truck and see if he would take me to my car. My plan was to follow truck ruts to Buffalo, 40 miles away.

Finally, I saw a truck approaching. I ran out to meet it with a sandwich in one hand and a car brush in the other. I waved the truck down and told the driver my dilemma. Could he take me to my car? He was reluctant, but he was familiar with the area and finally agreed to do it.

After a couple miles, we saw the blinking lights of my car. He stopped behind it. I brushed the snow off of it. Then the driver slowly moved his truck around me and I followed him back to Route 20, where he left me in his wake. I proceeded to drive about five or six miles per hour for the next six or seven hours, following the truck's ruts, praying all the way, making deals with God. After six or seven miles, I saw the golden arches of a McDonald's. I realized I was back in civilization, in a suburb of Buffalo that had left the lights on.

I reached I-90 east of Buffalo. The road was open. I got to Rochester at 4 o'clock in the morning. Though I was tired and needed rest—I had an interview scheduled at my hotel at 7 o'clock with a player and his coach—I couldn't sleep because I couldn't stop shaking. My feet still had no feeling. I had never endured anything comparable to my near-death experience that Sunday. For 15 terrifying hours, lost in that fierce winter snowstorm, I thought I was going to die. I couldn't stop thinking about how I should go out and enjoy life and do things and be more of a well-rounded person. I kept thinking about the promises I had made to God while in my car. I wanted to keep those promises.

The next day, the player and coach arrived on time to our interview, even though the airports and schools were closed due to the storm. That we all managed to be there, I knew, was something of a miracle.

POSTGAME SUMMARY

23

POSTGAME SUMMARY

IN ALMOST 30 YEARS OF TRAVELING through the United States to evaluate thousands of high school football players, Tom Lemming has met hundreds of high school and college coaches, visited hundreds of historic sites, and dined at hundreds of restaurants. Here are some lists of his favorites:

1. TOP 11 COLLEGE RECRUITERS (HEAD COACHES):
    1. Pete Carroll, USC
    2. Phil Fulmer, Tennessee
    3. Mack Brown, Texas
    4. Lloyd Carr, Michigan
    5. Charlie Weis, Notre Dame
    6. Ed Orgeron, Mississippi
    7. Bobby Bowden, Florida State
    8. Joe Paterno, Penn State
    9. Jimmy Johnson, Miami (Florida)
    10. Barry Alvarez, Wisconsin
    11. Jim Tressel, Ohio State

2. TOP 11 COLLEGE RECRUITERS (ASSISTANTS):

1. John Blake, Nebraska/North Carolina
2. Lane Kiffin, USC
3. Tim Brewster, North Carolina/Texas
4. Doc Holiday, Florida
5. Kevin Steele, Alabama
6. Larry Johnson, Penn State
7. Rob Ianello, Wisconsin/Notre Dame
8. Mike DeBord, Michigan
9. Ron English, Michigan
10. Greg McMahon, Illinois
11. Dave Roberts, Vanderbilt/South Carolina

3. TOP 11 COLLEGE RECRUITING COORDINATORS:

1. Vinny Cerrato, Notre Dame
2. Jerry Pettibone, Oklahoma/Nebraska
3. Bill Rees, UCLA
4. Bill Conley, Ohio State
5. Bob Pitard, Georgia
6. Jerry Petercuskie, North Carolina State
7. Bob Chmiel, Michigan
8. Ronnie Cottrell, Florida State
9. Mike Heywood, LSU/Texas
10. Tim Cassidy, Texas A&M
11. Chris LaSalla, Pittsburgh

4. MY ALL-TIME RECRUITING TEAM (OFFENSE):

Year	Player	Position
1994	Tony Gonzalez	TE
1995	Randy Moss	WR
1984	Cris Carter	WR
1993	Orlando Pace	OL
1992	Jon Ogden	OL
1981	Bill Fralic	OL
1992	Korey Stringer	OL
2003	Jeff Byers	OL
1979	John Elway	QB
2003	Adrian Peterson	RB
1987	Emmitt Smith	RB
1980	Herschel Walker	RB

5. MY ALL-TIME RECRUITING TEAM (DEFENSE):

Year	Player	Position
1979	George Achica	DL
1994	Darrell Russell	DL
1988	Alonzo Spellman	DL
1997	Hubert Thompson	DL
1986	John Foley	LB
1989	Sean Gilbert	LB
1990	Derrick Brooks	LB
1996	LaVar Arrington	LB
1995	Charles Woodson	DB
1992	Bobby Taylor	DB
1983	Rod Woodson	DB
1992	Lawyer Milloy	DB

6. MY ANNUAL CHOICES AS THE NO. 1 PLAYER IN THE NATION:

YEAR	PLAYER	HOMETOWN	POSITION	COLLEGE
1979	John Elway	Granada Hills, CA	QB	Stanford
1980	Herschel Walker	Wrightsville, GA	RB	Georgia
1981	Bill Fralic	Pittsburgh, PA	OL	Pittsburgh
1982	Marcus Dupree	Philadelphia, MI	RB	Oklahoma
1983	Alvin Miller	Kirkwood, MO	WR	Notre Dame
1984	Chris Spielman	Massillon, OH	LB	Ohio State
1985	Hart Lee Dykes	Bay City, TX	WR	Oklahoma State
1986	Jeff George	Indianapolis, IN	QB	Purdue
1987	Emmitt Smith	Pensacola, FL	RB	Florida
1988	Todd Collins	Dandridge, TN	LB	Michigan
1989	Sean Gilbert	Aliquippa, PA	LB	Pittsburgh
1990	Jerome Bettis	Detroit, MI	RB	Notre Dame
1991	KiJana Carter	Westerville, OH	RB	Penn State
1992	Steve Davis	Spartanburg, SC	RB	Auburn
1993	Ron Powlus	Berwick, PA	QB	Notre Dame
1994(tie)	Peyton Manning	New Orleans, LA	QB	Tennessee
And	Josh Booty	Shreveport, LA	QB	LSU
1995	Randy Moss	Belle DuPont, WV	WR	Marshall
1996	Tim Couch	Hyden, KY	QB	Kentucky
1997	LaVar Arrington	Pittsburgh, PA	LB	Penn State
1998	Drew Henson	Brighton, MI	QB	Michigan
1999	Chris Simms	Franklin Lakes, NJ	QB	Texas
2000	Charlie Rogers	Saginaw, MI	WR	Michigan State
2001	Joe Mauer	St. Paul, MN	QB	Florida State
2002	Ben Olson	Thousand Oaks, CA	QB	Brigham Young
2003	Chris Leak	Charlotte, NC	QB	Florida
2004	Adrian Peterson	Palestine, TX	RB	Oklahoma
2005	Ryan Perrilloux	Reserve, LA	QB	LSU
2006	Chris Wells	Akron, OH	RB	Ohio State
2007	Jimmy Clausen	Westlake Village, CA	QB	Notre Dame

7. MY FIVE FAVORITE PLACES TO VISIT ON MY ANNUAL ROAD TRIP:
1. San Antonio, Texas
2. Boston, Massachusetts
3. Washington, D.C.
4. Clearwater, Florida
5. Gueydan, Louisiana

8. MY FIVE FAVORITE PLACES TO EAT ON MY ANNUAL ROAD TRIP:
1. Merchant's Café, Seattle, Washington
2. Trattoria Pomigliano, Libertyville, Illinois
3. Pat O'Brien's, San Antonio, Texas
4. Creole Kitchen, Gueydan, Louisiana
5. Calhoun's on the River, Knoxville, Tennessee

9. TOP 11 HIGH SCHOOL COACHES WHO DO THE MOST FOR THEIR PLAYERS:
1. George Smith, Aquinas High School, Fort Lauderdale, Florida
2. Gary Korhonen, Richards High School, Oak Lawn, Illinois
3. Bill McGregor, DeMatha High School, Hyattsville, Maryland
4. Ted Ginn, Sr., Glenville High School, Cleveland, Ohio
5. Greg Toal, Don Bosco High School, Ramsey, New Jersey
6. John Wrenn, Hamilton High School, Chandler, Arizona
7. Dave White, Bishop Gorman High School, Las Vegas, Nevada
8. John Curtis, John Curtis High School, River Ridge, Louisiana
9. Ricky Woods, South Panola High School, Batesville, Mississippi
10. Jon Mack, St. Bonaventure High School, Ventura, California
11. Jay Frye, Richland Southeast High School, Columbia, South Carolina

10. TOP FIVE PLACES I HAVEN'T HAD TIME TO VISIT BUT PLAN TO:
    1. Grand Canyon, Arizona
    2. Little Big Horn, Montana
    3. Monument Valley, Arizona
    4. Mount Rushmore, South Dakota
    5. Redwood Forest, California

Index

W

Y

Z

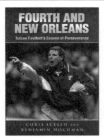